Supporting Literacy

Developing Effective Learning Environments

Supporting Literacy

Developing Effective Learning Environments

Catherine E. Loughlin
Mavis D. Martin

Foreword by Yetta M. Goodman

Teachers College, Columbia University
New York and London

Published by Teachers College Press, 1234 Amsterdam Avenue, New York, NY 10027

Library of Congress Cataloging-in-Publication Data

Loughlin, Catherine E., 1927–
  Supporting literacy.

  Bibliography: p.
  Includes index.
  1. Reading (Elementary) 2. Language arts
(Elementary) 3. Classroom environment. 4. Teacher-
student relationships. 5. Literacy. I. Martin, Mavis D.,
1926–   . II. Title.
LB1573.L64 1987   372.4   87-1964
ISBN 0-8077-2859-4

Illustrations by Robert Jason Lee

Manufactured in the United States of America

92 91 90 89 88   2 3 4 5 6

Dedicated to the memory of
Marie M. Hughes
A Teacher

Contents

Foreword

The classroom is greater than the sum of its parts. The classroom is more than one child plus one child plus one child. It is a community.

There is a new child study movement in education these days. Researchers are spending their time observing in classrooms to describe the interrelations among teachers, students, and their daily environment. Others are talking about the classroom as a community that can be studied with some of the same techniques used by sociologists and anthropologists, who study other kinds of human communities. Piagetians are discussing collaborative learning in classrooms and Vygotskians are focusing on the impact of the social aspects of the classroom on individual learning.

After a number of decades of research focusing on individual learners as if they were isolated from others, concern has once again turned to issues related to the classroom community as a social entity.

At the same time, many scholars concerned with literacy have begun to question such notions as reading readiness, learning to read before reading to learn, and didactic teaching of reading and writing. Based on these notions, instructional activities have been planned as if elementary school students are learning literacy in a vacuum, totally divorced from the highly literate society in which they participate daily. But evidence is accumulating that children are not blank slates when it comes to knowledge about written language. By the time they come to school, children know how to handle books and newspapers differentially. They know how to use writing implements of all kinds. They know that stories often start with "Once upon a time" and that letters start with "Dear Somebody." They know the importance of their name in a world of other important names.

Teachers and administrators who are looking for ways to respond to the new knowledge coming from research on literacy learning in the classroom and on improving the quality of teaching will find *Sup-*

porting Literacy: Developing Effective Learning Environments very useful. It is obvious that Catherine Loughlin and Mavis Martin are no strangers to classrooms. The specifics they provide could only have been presented by educators who have spent years studying classroom environments, literacy, teachers, and children and who know how these can be interrelated to organize a rich literacy setting in which students learn to read and write at the same time they are reading and writing to learn. At the same time, school personnel have been searching for ways to control the behavior of students in classrooms, resorting in most cases to the autocratic imposition of simplistic devices such as rewards and punishment for children. The ideas presented in this book, on the other hand, suggest that behavior is a result of the ways in which schools and classrooms are organized and curricula are developed.

Organizing a classroom while keeping in mind how students learn, the problems they need and want to solve, and the literacy learning that helps them solve their problems places the management of the classroom into a collaborative arena. Students are as concerned with how their classrooms run as their teachers are, and all members of the classroom community become involved with self-management, self-evaluation, and self-control.

Quiet, neat classrooms with little visible print do not provide a setting in which children can explore written language. Didactic teaching does not provide the opportunity for the risk taking necessary for children to discover the flexibility, conventionality, and power of reading and writing. Formal reading and writing lessons do not provide students with the opportunity to explore the many functions written language serves in their daily lives.

Those of us who believe that classrooms need to provide daily living and learning experiences that invite children to participate in a literate community will find that this handbook is organized to allow children to inquire into literacy, to use literacy, and to take the necessary risks related to its use. It is not necessary to agree with all the ideas presented or to put into practice every suggestion. The intent of the book is to get teachers and teacher educators to observe classrooms with new knowledge about learning environments and literacy learning and then to organize a classroom literacy community based on their developing practical theory about literacy environments. This provocative resource will aid teachers in such an important endeavor.

YETTA M. GOODMAN
Program in Language and Literacy
The University of Arizona

Preface

In this book about the environment and literacy, two bodies of work come together: studies of the physical environment of the classroom and its profound influence on behavior and studies of the acquisition of literacy. This information offers considerable direction to teachers for the development of the learning environment as a tool on behalf of children's growth in literacy. The environmental principles and arrangements described are much more than a simple addendum to a reading and language-arts instructional program.

Environmental influences are always present in the classroom. Arranging a functional literacy environment entails an intentional directing of those influences to promote established goals. The literature on acquisition of literacy helps us identify the contexts and reading behaviors we wish to see occurring in the classroom, while information about the environment-behavior relationship suggests specific arrangements most likely to bring about those contexts and behaviors. Together these reveal an environment that recognizes children construct their own language growth, reflects meaning in the fullest sense of personal and cultural relevance, matches individual levels of ability, and supports self-initiated literacy activity.

The principles and arrangements we describe are based on an examination of the environment's influence and the identification of specific arrangements to stimulate spontaneous literacy behaviors in children. This book examines a special use of the environment and does not present all the available environmental data from which these practices derive. More information about the influences of the environmental elements of spatial organization, provisioning, and materials arrangement on a broader variety of classroom events than those related to literacy is discussed in *The Learning Environment: An Instructional Strategy* (Loughlin & Suina, 1982).

Our extensive experiences with in-service programs have shown us that an awareness of the direct relationship between environment and children's behaviors and learning is not typically included in a teacher's frame of reference about the teaching-learning process. Classrooms are generally arranged for aesthetic or housekeeping purposes. As a result, it is difficult for many teachers to see the almost unlimited possibilities for strong, continuing independent influences that exist, outside the contexts of lessons, within the physical environment of the classroom.

We have, consequently, become involved in trying to help teachers see, describe, and understand the differences between displaying print and organizing working elements of a functional literacy environment. It has been our experience that these differences are genuine, but that they encompass concepts hard to discern. We have seen teachers become fascinated by working with these challenges, and we believe this book can help teachers understand and use the environment to extend their teaching strategies for literacy.

The environmental examples we use here to illustrate the elements of the functioning literacy environment are authentic. We have been fortunate to work in a large number of classrooms where teachers have understood the role of environment and effectively arranged it to encourage and support children's literacy, and we share their environmental designs through descriptions and illustrations.

The words *functioning* and *environment* as they are used here have technical meaning. The physical environment—its arrangement and its contents—is of major concern. And there is an emphasis on the functioning of the environment, and the role of the teacher in activating and managing that functioning, to assist children in their literacy acquisition. From this perspective, we discuss ways to organize time and events to provide access to the literacy stimuli of the environment, the effects of a teacher-modeled response to the environment, organization of routines that take advantage of environmental literacy opportunities, and the involvement of learners in the ongoing maintenance of current literacy.

This practical approach builds upon the framework for the acquisition of language and literacy, which is rooted in the home and community, and continues into the planned and unplanned elements of school life. The theoretical position and the practical explications thus function as a whole, making this a work that can be both a handbook for the classroom practitioner and a provocative study resource for the teacher of teachers.

Supporting Literacy

Developing Effective Learning Environments

1

The Functioning Literacy Environment

The framework for the functioning literacy environment is found in the interface of two bodies of knowledge, that of the learning environment and that of the acquisition of literacy, as they are applied to the same question: How can the environment support the development and continuous uses of literacy? Understanding the environment-behavior relationship enables teachers to provision and organize so that desired literacy behaviors are likely to occur. Knowledge of the process of literacy acquisition makes it possible to identify those desired literacy behaviors.

The physical environment of the classroom can be a powerful tool at the disposal of the teacher or it can be an unrecognized and undirected influence on behavior and learning. Informed knowledge about environmental principles, combined with clearly defined teaching purposes, enables teachers to arrange environments that reflect and extend their instructional work with children (Loughlin & Suina, 1982).

The curriculum for literacy is an unquestioned priority in the elementary school today, whether it is called literacy, reading, language arts, or something else. Environmental principles applied to curriculum goals can enhance literacy growth by producing settings arranged to offer purpose for literacy, focus on the meanings of print, capture children's interest in literacy activity, and so increase the spontaneous use of literacy throughout the day.

LANGUAGE ACQUISITION AND ITS CONTEXT

The concept of the functioning literacy environment implies that there are resources, activities, and behaviors within environments that directly influence the literacy process. Understanding this relationship requires recognition that literacy is a part of the entire complex process of language, that literacy growth is part of the acquisition of language, and that utility in the daily lives of learners offers motivation for both oral language and literacy acquisition.

Oral Language Acquisition

Learning oral language is an astonishing achievement of very young children; almost all learn to speak their mother tongue. Oral language development precedes and parallels literacy development, and there are some elements widely accepted as essential in the language acquisition process that have implications for environments designed to support literacy development.

Children learn their own language without formal instruction, and it is generally accepted that children construct their own language themselves, from the sounds they hear and the uses they see in an ongoing interaction with their surroundings. While every infant has the potentiality for learning any language, what is learned is what is heard. However, infants do not simply imitate what they hear. No two children, even in the same environment, hear or use precisely the same content and expressions. Language appears as a personal expression of their own needs and motivation. Children use their early language for a variety of purposes, but always in a personal fashion, dictated by individual interaction with environmental stimuli.

While making increasingly accurate efforts to reproduce the sounds and the language style used, repeated, and stressed by the surrounding caretakers, the infant tries out a variety of sounds and creates his own syntax, content, and style. At this stage there is a lot of trial and error in the language production. This creative language beginner takes risks and is guided throughout by the effort to establish communication with others in the environment in some sensible fashion.

It is generally acknowledged that immersion in language environment is essential for language acquisition (Smith, 1972), but this development must be triggered by influences in the child's environment. Cazden calls this type of influence "environmental assistance" (Cazden, 1972). Children are purposeful when learning a language, and the entire process is interactive. The environment provides both the language models and the personal motivation to keep the child involved and to provide stimulating responses. Language learners talk because they want to tell someone their needs, interact with someone, express themselves, ask for or give information.

Some Conditions for Language Acquisition

- Environmental stimuli and modeling
- Interaction opportunities
- Purpose and meaning
- Practice
- Adult tolerance for trial and error

Children learn their language by using it. They grasp everything that feeds into their effort, and they move steadily toward increasing order and accuracy as they build toward a logic and stability in all aspects of oral language. This may or may not be the language of the larger community and the school. It may even be that the child is learning more than one language. Whatever the circumstance, language learning can be seen as a process that is continuous, interactive, meaning-focused, and creative (Lindfors, 1985).

One of the most obvious characteristics of language is that it is purposeful. The purposes for which people use language seem unlimited. Halliday (1973) and Clark, Moran, and Burrows (1981) have categorized different functions of language. Smith (1983) discussed literacy and nonlanguage behaviors that could serve the same functions as oral language, but suggested that the term *functions* tends to detract from the extreme flexibility with which language and literacy can be employed. Language tends to be acquired and extended within a framework of social purposes.

Literacy Acquisition

The principles of language acquisition, whether in the development of oral language or in the development of reading and writing competencies, are generally accepted as being similar, though the form may be different. Many adults think of their own literacy as a simple matter of "learning to read"—being taught to read—at school. Today, however, literacy acquisition can be seen as part of a process that is much broader and potentially more spontaneous than formal reading instruction. There is a physical, graphic dimension to literacy, and in societies where the community communicates through those symbols, there is considerable evidence that young children begin to understand the purposes and meaning of print encountered in their environment before they begin school (Clark, 1976).

It appears that the roots of literacy are cultivated much earlier in a child's life than was once thought. This revised opinion comes from a view of literacy as a part of the broad-spectrum whole-language context and from increased awareness of the writing and reading of preschool children. For educational purposes it is helpful to realize that the use of language in its written form begins long before school instruction and is shaped by many influences other than direct instruction (Clay, 1972; Holdaway, 1979). Literacy is a dimension of language, rather than an entirely different and separate process. In the development of reading and writing, speaking and listening, each draws on sensible awareness of language purposes and potentials in the environment as part of the integrated language process in the home and community.

Observation of children's earliest reading and writing shows literacy as a social interaction, frequently a companion to oral events in the home and community. Case studies describe the reading of some three-year-olds as being functional and social, as is their oral language (Baghban, 1984).

Some preschool children recognize many print symbols, from animated Sesame Street alphabets to formal primers, and hundreds of commercial trademarks are in the print repertoires of many children. Descriptive research studies (Taylor, 1983) show children involved in the print of their mother's shopping lists; the reading of traffic signs; the recognition of food, candy, and other household packages; the creating of their own words with magnetic letters on refrigerator doors; and the writing of titles or stories for their own art work. While this description applies to many children, it does not apply to all schoolchildren. Not all communities, not all families are literate to the same extent. Books, advertisements, and letters are so commonly seen in some homes that children find it very natural to use the same kinds of print at school. Other children have little or no experience with print in their homes or communities. Some see adults making frequent use of functional print; others don't see their important adults using print very much.

Quantitative differences in the environment are not the only significant variations. There are wide differences in literacy sources and application. Some children observe extensive use of libraries and personally owned books for both pleasure and practical purposes. Others may see books used mainly as practical resources. Still others may see frequent reading from periodicals but little from books. Some are familiar with a high level of production of personal writing, from lists to letters, while others are not accustomed to any kind of family production of print.

Demand for use of literacy can vary by community and by culture. In some places supermarket bulletin boards offer almost every conceivable item for sale, and crowds gather to read these ads; in others bulletin boards offer only job-wanted notices and only occasionally does one see a reader there. In some households all recipes are in print, and children see them rewritten to be shared with others; other children have never seen a recipe written. In some communities religious ritual and songs are codified in an order of worship and a hymnal; in others the worship style of centuries remains oral and inherited and has never been written. The school's literacy environment supports the child's move from oral language and home literacy to school literacy by reflecting the purposes for which print is used at home and by associating print with content about the home, whether or not literacy is an important part of the home and community. For some children the print may be strange, but the content will be familiar. By reflecting the home and the community this way, the environment builds connections, offering a personal context for each child. To establish those connections it is important to know which things are customarily written and which are not, and it is equally important to know what community information its members consider appropriate for others to know.

Early and personal literacy support in the school environment resembles the environmental support for early oral language learning that surrounds the child in the home. In each case the environment supplies a continuous, interactive, meaning-focused opportunity for the use of language in one of its forms, within a social milieu in which the child is comfortable.

Growth in literacy is not limited by purpose, age, or achievement of a given set of competencies. A mature reader continues to add focus and expand literacy abilities throughout life. Habits involving recreational and practical use of print may be established early and used in continuous growth. A functioning literacy environment provides the circumstances that enhance literacy growth through the years of schooling. There are, of course, many programs that apply directly to the teaching of reading and writing, and the role of the environment is to support and complement teachers' instructional efforts. Contemporary views of language acquisition and literacy development, with their emphasis on environment, provide important insights into the nature of the functioning literacy environment.

THE ARRANGED ENVIRONMENT

The term *learning environment* has many different meanings. It has been defined as any single variable or combination of variables of the built, the natural, or the arranged environment, and as the social, psychological, institutional, and management aspects of settings for learning. However, of all of these, the concept of the *arranged environment* provides more useful information than any other for the development of the functional literacy environment (Loughlin, 1978).

The architectural facility and the arranged environment are the major components of the physical learning environment. Each plays a different role, with different functions and characteristics. The architectural facility establishes qualities of the basic setting and access to external spaces and resources, but the active and responsive elements of the learning environment are arranged by teachers within the spaces and settings provided by the architectural design and construction. The arranged environment is the part of the physical environment arranged by teachers, including all spaces organized through furniture placement, all learning materials selected and placed in the environment, and arrangement of those materials for the learners' use. It is not hard to arrange good learning environments in those settings where the architectural facility has been designed for the particular program it houses. However, knowledgeable teachers can arrange environments that are harmonious with program style and purposes even in more difficult architectural settings when they are aware of environmental influences on behavior and learning and can apply their knowledge to the tasks of environmental arrangement.

Each teacher-arranged environment is unique, appropriate for the individuals for whom it is arranged, and responsive to the changing needs and activities associated with children's growth. The arranged environment functions as an instructional tool, complementing and reinforcing other strategies the teacher uses to support children's learning.

The Children's Environment

Because of differences in size, role, movement patterns, and experience background, adults and children have different visual and spatial experiences in the same environment; they occupy different spaces, see different surroundings, and perceive the content of the environment differently (Loughlin, 1977).

The children's environment consists of the spaces they occupy, the materials they can touch and use, and the materials and information perceived as they visually scan the area. Their environment doesn't include the space above their heads or any objects there, except when somebody directs their attention to them.

The adults' environment includes materials and spaces they see, the stored materials organized out of sight, and an overview of the total environment. Unlike children, adults are very much aware of objects or surfaces two to three feet above eye level and tend to overlook spaces below their knees.

The distinction between the adult environment and the child environment is an important one. Adults see the environment as it actually exists for children and as it influences and shapes their activity only when they move into the spaces where children settle or move and can scan the area from the children's eye level. If they move from the adults' to the children's environment and train themselves to consider the children's view of the space, teachers can better understand the classroom events associated with environmental arrangements.

The Environment-Behavior Relationship

The physical surroundings of the learning environment shape the behaviors of children and teachers by giving very strong messages, encouraging them to act in particular ways. Messages urge movement in this direction or that, suggest noticing some materials more than others, encourage interaction with or isolation from other people. Environmental messages may suggest hurried, calm, or excited movements, encourage putting certain materials together, or invite discussion.

With or without the awareness of the teacher, the environment sends messages and children respond. Environmental messages are extremely powerful, and sometimes teachers are unaware that they have provoked unwanted behaviors by environmental arrangements. Puzzling behaviors can often be understood when environmental information is used to examine the settings in which those behaviors are seen. Examining materials arrangements, with the understanding that the location of provisions influence their use, can show why children seem to ignore materials the teacher thought would be popular. A simple but deliberate rearrangement of materials can change an unwanted behavior pattern. Knowledge of the environment-behavior relationship is especially powerful as a tool when used to design arrangements to encourage behaviors considered conducive to learning. While one teacher unintentionally arranges an environment in which children appear to be completely uninterested in books, another, with similar space and materials, can thoughtfully arrange one where children are constantly drawn to reading. The difference is in the application of environmental principles and a clear understanding of the power of physical surroundings to shape what children do.

Environmental Tasks

There are three basic tasks involved in arranging the learning environment within the architectural facility. These tasks are spatial organization, provisioning, and materials arrangement. A fourth environmental task, organizing for special purposes, calls upon teachers to apply knowledge of the other three tasks as they arrange environments to promote particular teaching purposes or behavior expectations.

Spatial organization is the task of arranging furniture to create spaces for movement and learning activities. Those spaces affect many classroom behaviors, such as attention span, quality of language interaction, and uses of materials. Spatial organization shapes the quality and the direction of movement and determines which spaces are used.

Provisioning for learning is the task of placing materials and equipment in the environment to enable children to get on with their learning activities. Teachers choose and gather learning materials and determine timing and context for their introduction into the environment.

The environment's provisions shape the content and form of the learning activities that can occur within that environment and also have a long-term effect on learning outcomes, influencing the knowledge, skills, and thinking processes developed as children use the environment.

Several basic categories of essential provisions support activities in any environment (Loughlin & Suina, 1982). Access to provisions from these categories enables children to sustain involvement and show independence in productive learning activities. In addition, the particular objects and materials selected for each provisioning category establish the specific learning potential of the environment and affect its ability to engage and hold children's interest.

Materials arrangement consists of organization, display, and placement of learning materials. Clear display highlights learning materials and their attributes, sending children continuous suggestions for learning activities. Materials arranged for physical access enable children to locate, use, and replace materials independently. Materials arrangement affects attention span, apparent material preferences, and the ways materials are used. Teacher-planned combinations of materials shape the kinds of learning activities initiated and the skills children are most likely to practice on their own.

Organizing for special purposes is a task in which teachers apply everything they know about spatial organization, provisioning, and materials arrangement and their relationships to children's behaviors. The knowledge can be applied to any special instructional purpose, as long as the relevant classroom events and behaviors can be clarified. When a special purpose, such as promoting the spontaneous use of books, has been identified, a teacher can deliberately make those environmental arrangements most associated with the desired events.

The same environmental principles, applied to various programs and purposes, enable teachers to build into their environments such diverse purposes as the development of cooperative group work skills, meeting the mobility needs of special children, increasing attention span, encouraging experimentation, and promoting literacy. These and many other special purposes can be supported by the arranged environment, as teachers carry out the tasks of spatial organization, provisioning, and materials arrangement with those purposes clearly in mind.

Because the arranged environment stimulates and facilitates physical actions and behaviors of learners, it isn't useful to plan environmental arrangements entirely in terms of subjects, concepts, or ideas to be learned. Environments can support children as they observe, build, write, handle books, chart, measure, or stack objects, but children don't really fraction, art, phonic, or science (Rambusch, 1971). Environmental arrangements are best designed on the basis of what seems important for children to *do*, in a physical sense, in relation to particular instructional purposes.

Special Purposes for the Literacy Environment

The processes of oral language acquisition and literacy acquisition suggest that just as language development is stimulated within the pervasive language environment of infants, the move toward literacy is stimulated in surroundings where symbols and print are an important part of daily living. The development of language and literacy has strong dimensions of purpose and meaning. The desire to grasp or express important personal meaning moves the language learner, either writer or reader, to use those forms of language, and it is through use that language and literacy grow. The classroom environment also plays a part in the development of literacy, and a key role of the functioning literacy environment is surrounding children with symbols and print, making the literacy environment as constant and pervasive as the oral-language environment. Another role is to stimulate spontaneous uses of a variety of literacy behaviors for purposes that have meaning for children. More specific purposes for the environment's support of literacy can be identified from descriptions of the experiences known to foster children's growth in literacy.

Organizing for Special Purposes
Children's Literacy Activities

- Using symbols for own purposes
- Encountering models of written communication
- Using print to negotiate the day
- Practicing literacy through use
- Finding reason to gain literacy competence
- Communicating through print
- Taking risks with print
- Focusing on meaning
- Using literacy for social interaction
- Finding print associated with important events and people

As they arrange the literacy environment, teachers consider both the experiences associated with growth in literacy and the conditions needed to support those experiences. They plan their environmental arrangement carefully with those considerations in mind. For example, teachers want children to use symbols and print to negotiate the school day and to encounter many models of written communication, experiencing the need and opportunity to gain further competence in literacy, so they offer procedural information primarily in graphic and print form. In addition, they display print and other symbolic information with great clarity, so that it is always noticeable and readable.

THE LEARNING ENVIRONMENT AND LITERACY

The studies of literacy in classroom environments offer descriptions of teacher-arranged environments for literacy (Cole & Loughlin, 1984) and describe conditions under which children make extensive use of the literacy environment. The observations of those studies reveal children's uses of the environment's literacy, teachers' environmental work in maintaining high levels of literacy, and children's literacy behaviors.

Characteristics of the Literacy Environment

No matter how unique the specific arrangements for literacy in individual classrooms, there are some common characteristics in all the literacy environments studied. First among these is the evident use of literacy by all adults and children as a normal, active way of life. Print and symbols offer information and direction, rather than simply advertising print. Wherever there is stimulus for the use of literacy, the means to respond are present. Several other elements are also important in suggesting and supporting extensive uses of literacy when children are not directly engaged with the teacher or involved in teacher-assigned activities.

The Functioning Literacy Environment

- Interesting things
- Recording tools and recording materials
- Places to settle down
- Books everywhere
- References
- Display space and display tools
- Time and opportunity

Interesting things to read and write about focus the activities that prompt children to read and write. Animals, artifacts, machines, models, and other concrete information sources provide firsthand, rather than symbolic, encounters with information, ideas, or knowledge. Other, more symbolic information sources, such as pictures, charts, diagrams, articles, and books, are also present, offering reasons to read more, take notes, share information with others. Combinations of print and nonprint information capitalize on the capacity of the concrete to engage children in activity, establish interest, and lead the learners to seek and record information in symbolic form.

Recording tools and materials, in every area where children work, ensure that stimulus and opportunity for writing are present when and wherever children find something to write about. Placing tools and materials for recording in the vicinity of working children markedly increases the extent of spontaneous record keeping and writing that occur within the environment.

Varied places to settle down for reading and writing lend support to the suggestions to record and to seek useful information from print. Places to sit, to stop and make a quick note, to discuss what is being read or what is being written, and to work alone all support the uses of literacy for different and individual purposes, increasing the likelihood that the impulse to write and read will be followed with action.

Books everywhere in the functioning literacy environment keep involvement and interest in literature strong. A few books in every area leave room for other materials, which in turn call attention to books whose contents are related to the materials. In some areas books offer information to help children in their activities in that space. In other areas books are highlighted for their seasonal content, and in others for the ways they reflect, and offer insights into, children's lives. Books are displayed so children are aware of them as they glance about. These arrangements encourage children to turn to books again and again in the course of the day as they engage in the spontaneous uses of literacy.

References where needed are important, as children attempt to record, share, communicate, or make announcements through print. References in a variety of forms are among the most used resources in the functioning literacy environment because they are present everywhere. Children who respond to the stimulus for writing need information about written language to get their message or ideas into print. In the urgency of getting ideas written, children use whatever resources are nearby.

Display spaces and tools, available in all areas of the environment, are an essential support for communication. They stimulate children's interest in the ideas and projects of others and give a context for the self-initiated use of literacy for preparing and labeling personal displays or examining the displays of classmates. Children's display of their own work and writing results in direct, objective feedback about the need for print conventions and legibility in their writing. Available display spaces and tools help keep messages current, so children attend to displayed print and act upon it. The widely available spaces and tools for display keep the literacy environment growing and changing and make literacy an important part of daily living.

Time and opportunity to respond to the stimulus for literacy, which is encountered again and again in the literacy environment, are the elements that make all other environmental arrangements function. Physical access to all materials, time to become engaged with the literacy of the environment, and the right to display one's own work verify the genuineness of literacy invitations and enable children to grow in literacy through their own efforts.

Providing Access to Displayed Literacy

It may seem obvious that carefully arranged literacy stimuli cannot promote literacy growth unless children are permitted to make use of them, but it's easy to overlook that last step in establishing the functioning literacy environment. In some classrooms more uses of literacy materials were seen during transitions and free time (recess, lunchtime) than other periods of the day, even including some time blocks devoted to literacy activities (Loughlin & Ivener, 1984). It is as though children wait for a chance to get to the tools, materials, and print messages of the environment, then use them as quickly as they can while the opportunity exists. Observers also see some furtive uses of literacy at times when it is not on the instructional agenda. It appears that although the displayed print and other literacy materials encourage children to become engaged with literacy activity, the requirements of the day have priority. There are so many obligations there is little time left for personal response to environmental literacy invitations. Observations of other classrooms show more use of the environment's literacy materials throughout the day.

The presence of a variety of literacy stimuli is extremely important, but access is also essential. The functioning literacy environment is not fully arranged until the day is organized to provide opportunities for response to those stimuli.

Ways of Providing Access

- Schedule Self-selection Time
- Extending Transitions
- Organizing Flexible Time Blocks
- Offering Options Within Activities
- Using Environment for Direct Interaction

TEACHERS AND THE LITERACY ENVIRONMENT

The work of a teacher is extensive and complex, and within the framework of literacy at least two different roles can be described. The instructional role, which is the most visible, involves teachers in planning learning experiences for literacy, working directly with children, and assigning and supervising independent literacy activities.

Equally important, but more subtle, is the teacher's environmental role, which is less well known. Carrying out this role involves teachers in the establishment of the literacy environment and as a catalyst to initiate and maintain its functioning so that children's literacy growth continues throughout the time children are in the environment. The role can be described in terms of what teachers decide *about* the environment, what they do *to* the environment behind the scenes, and what they do *in* the environment while the children are there (Martin & Loughlin, 1976).

Decisions About the Environment

A large quantity of current displayed print is required to keep a group of active learners involved in spontaneous literacy activities. Selecting, displaying, and rotating all displayed print to keep it current is an enormous job for one person. Such tasks can be overwhelming, but teachers observed in their environmental role share the responsibility for the display of print with children. First, they decide to share ownership of the environment, including display spaces often saved for the teacher. They make those places available to everyone and provision nearby areas with materials and tools to help children display well.

In the literacy environment teachers share responsibility for dispensing provisions for children's use. Rather than personally handing out materials, they share plans for distributing those provisions, enabling children to check and replenish all supplies, keeping the environment ready for all the day's literacy activities. Inventory lists help children find out what provisions are needed and show where they are available. These same lists provoke genuine purpose for literacy behaviors as children participate in the maintenance of the environment.

In addition to sharing ownership and responsibility for the environment, the teachers also share information, displaying in print the information they formerly doled out as the day progressed. Information about groupings, directions, schedules, descriptions of activities, visitors, lunch menus, and other events of the day belongs to everyone in the environment and is displayed in print so it can be consulted throughout the day.

Decisions to share ownership, to share responsibility, and to share information lead toward another set of environmental decisions concerning access to the environment and its literacy resources. Literacy potential is increased by expecting literacy behaviors to become tools in children's self-directed activity and in maintenance of the literacy environment. But teachers are the ones who decide how to provide access to the environment, organizing the day so children have time and opportunity to take advantage of the literacy potential designed for them. Teachers approach this in different ways, so that there are many different arrangements for access to the literacy in the environment. Whatever the approach, the decision to provide access is crucial to the functioning of the literacy environment.

Behind the Scenes

The initial establishment of the literacy environment is an important part of the teacher's environmental role, but the environment changes daily, keeping pace with children's growth in literacy and their expanding interests, so the arranging is never finished. Every day, behind the scenes, teachers add and reorganize materials and space. They make environmental responses to children's observed interests and efforts. Written messages, invitations, and commentary; books, information, provisions for writing; displays, special arrangements, collections of information sources—all of these are tools teachers use to keep the environment alive. Some are placed in the environment and others removed. Still others are relocated, combined with new materials in new settings.

Also behind the scenes, the teachers sample the environment after the children leave, looking at the finished products, the projects in progress, the posted literacy work, the written responses to teacher invitations, and other materials children have added to the environment in the course of the day. Teachers gather information about individuals' abilities, interests, and growth by reviewing what children have done and how, the competence with which they work, where they display their products and projects, to whom their messages are addressed, how much they use literacy in their self-initiated work, and other data from the environment.

Within the Environment

While children are working in the environment, teachers add further stimuli to the use of literacy and keep the environment functioning. Teachers model the use of the environment, using its resources for reading, message posting, chart writing, and reference consulting; they

> # The Teacher's Environmental Role
>
> **Decisions About the Environment**
> Share Ownership
> Share Responsibility
> Share Information
> Provide Access
>
> **Behind the Scenes**
> Add
> Reorganize
> Sample
>
> **Within the Environment**
> Model
> Observe
> Interact with Children

deliberately seek out occasions for modeling literacy behavior, often choosing to carry out some routine preparation tasks during the school day so children can observe these uses of literacy. The modeling legitimizes the use of the environment, encouraging children's literacy activity.

Observation of children using the environment is an important part of the teacher's role, because it reveals the processes that are not always evident in children's final products. Even brief observations of children's approaches to writing, their ways of selecting books, the ideas discussed before products take form, or their attempts to find specific information give new insights into their interests and abilities. Using this information, teachers make more effective responses to further stimulate involvement in literacy.

Moving through the literacy environment, teachers pause to ac-knowledge children's literacy efforts, point out materials, encourage collaboration, offer momentary assistance and consultation, or pro-vide some pertinent material not present in the area. These brief interactions help some children get started, encourage others to be persistent, and help still others find new directions for their literacy activities. Although brief, these interactions are effective because they are in the context of children's activity and are relevant to the child's purpose at the moment (Hughes, 1975), building on the strong tie between purpose, context, and the development of literacy.

OUTCOMES OF THE LITERACY ENVIRONMENT

Teachers who spend their days with children in well-developed literacy environments describe the environment's influences on the quantity and the quality of children's participation in literacy. Environmental arrangements make suggestions for literacy activity, encouraging children to think about extension of activity into some form of related literacy. Planned distribution of provisions enables children to follow those ideas through. Children's self-directed involvement with literacy is frequent and varied and at a much higher level than possible without supportive arrangements. Spontaneous writing is evident in functioning literacy environments. Children become involved with writing at their own levels of growth because they intend to express or convey some meaning or message. A corollary to the great interest in writing is a developing awareness of print conventions, leading toward the use of references and child-initiated editing and proofreading.

Perhaps connected to the amount of writing that occurs, the child-generated print displayed as a result, and the functional uses of print in the environment, there is a great deal of child-initiated reading activity related to seeking and verifying the meaning of print. Spontaneous reading is used at first for communication and information seeking; then other purposes develop along with a child's literacy abilities. Children make reading a part of any activity at any part of the day including recess and transition periods, putting to use all of the abilities currently available in a context that has purpose for them.

Because of the high level of reading activity in the literacy environment, there is an intensive involvement with books. Since books are everywhere their utility is readily seen, and their connection with children's lives and activities is emphasized by arrangement and display. Books are incorporated into most child-initiated activities in some way, as a resource or as a major focus for the activity, in social or solitary settings. Books are experienced as tools, sources of interesting information, and as literature. Through extensive and varied experiences, critical analysis and recognition of literary form develop and begin to influence writing as children continue to work within a functioning literacy environment (Van Dongen, 1984).

Literacy environment teachers describe some useful secondary outcomes of the environment arranged to promote literacy. There is strong self-direction and independence in the functioning literacy environment because information needed to work through the day is presented in print, so children are not dependent upon the teacher for every new action of the day. Carefully arranged provisions enable children to locate, use, and care for materials independently. The environment suggests activity, supports its completion, and continues to offer suggestions for other literacy activities. Sharing information about maintenance of the environment and other daily organization and routines reduces teacher time spent in presiding over the whole class during those routines.

Teachers also describe literacy environment influences on the curriculum. Because materials arrangement ensures that the suggestion for the use of literacy accompanies all provisions arranged anywhere in the environment, integration in the curriculum is inevitable. Whether the provisions are arranged in combinations suggesting science experimentation, or whether they stimulate some quantitative experience, literacy is part of the activity that occurs with those materials. The pattern of materials arrangement for literacy, which includes print and nonprint information, raw materials and tools, and recording provisions, also produces high interest among children. Given access to the environment and its provisions, children engaged in learning activity are supported in becoming self-directed, focused, and involved at a level not possible without the arrangements of the functioning literacy environment.

2

Provisioning for Literacy

An environment provisioned for literacy is first an environment provisioned for children's sustained learning activity. It offers a broad spectrum of materials to support children's involvement in learning and to provide a focus for literacy. Provisioning makes essential contributions to the environment's literacy characteristics that were presented in the previous chapter.

Provisions and their arrangements make it possible for children to work through the day with a great deal of independence and to make use of literacy throughout the day as a natural part of their activities. The literacy environment is self-perpetuating. Although it is initially provisioned by the teacher, it is maintained through daily use by those who work in the environment. Some responsibility for the production of displayed literacy is important for children's growth. Furthermore, to be practical, there just isn't time for teachers to produce and arrange all the print that keeps literacy alive for a diverse group during the course of a year. When provisioning supports children's production and display of print, there is a natural context for the uses and practice of literacy. This is as practical for children's growth as it is for the upkeep of the literacy level of the environment.

THE INVESTIGATION

The class was looking at a jellied cluster of round, black organisms in an aquarium. Some children were trying to identify them by reading a label on the container, but the words were unfamiliar. After a discussion of the organisms, Miss Ferro invited everyone to record hypotheses about their identity, so someone picked up chart paper and a marking pen from a shelf, took a roll of masking tape from the chalk ledge, and attached the chart paper to the wall. "They are eggs," she wrote. Then several other children added hypotheses while Josh, remembering a picture he had seen, leafed through two or three books near the aquarium, held one up, and told everybody there were illustrations of eggs in it.

Later, four children were still working on the question in a small area provisioned with paper and other raw materials, a tripod magnifying glass, and a low table with a microscope and two divided trays holding crayons, blank labels, strips of lined paper, scissors, pencils, marking pens, tacks, and glue. The children called Miss Ferro over to see one of the organisms crushed and smeared on a microscope slide, hoping that would help them get some useful information. After looking at it, she reminded the group about the school's bioscope, which could project the image of the microscope slide so everybody could see it at once, so somebody went to the office to borrow the instrument.

When the bioscope arrived, it was set up on the table with the barrel pointed down to project onto the table, and the slide was placed beneath the lens. The group saw that the slide was brown, but with a red area that surprised them. Was it part of the organism, or some problem with the slide?

After discussion of that, two children turned to the encyclopedia in the adjoining area and pulled out two volumes, sure they would find something about eggs, while somebody else, beside the bioscope, traced the red area on the projected image with a finger, then asked them to find some cross sections of eggs. One of the researchers checked the E volume, while the other looked in the F volume, then remembered a book on pond life in the library and went off to find it while the rest of the group stayed by the bioscope.

Then several things happened quickly. Somebody pointed to the projection from the bioscope, suggesting they outline it, another placed a piece of drawing paper under the bioscope and traced around the projected image with a pencil, and a third person used a crayon to show the color on the brown area. The researchers came back from the library and suggested showing the red areas on the drawing, so one of them lightly colored one area of the drawing red. The scissors from the table were used to cut around the circular outline of the drawing, and someone mounted it on dark backing while a label was written and then glued beneath the drawing.

The children helped one another return the tools and unused paper to their holders as the bioscope was packed in its case and the slide placed in the slide rack. Then they all moved to the meeting area, taking the mounted drawing with them.

From a distance, Miss Ferro noted that the group's work centered on the use of special equipment, but their activity was really sustained by the ordinary materials she had placed in the area. Print and nonprint information sources were available so everyone could be part of the group's investigation. When the children were ready to make a record of their findings, the raw materials to draw the projected image were close at hand, and the available tools for outlining and indicating color detail probably influenced the amount of information included in the observation record. When the group decided to share the observation record with other people, tools and materials in the area were used to prepare it for display. The provisions the teacher had placed in the area kept the process moving and sustained the children's involvement in their learning.

A PROVISIONING FRAMEWORK

Every classroom contains learning materials held in reserve for instructional sessions and other special purposes, and these materials play an important role in the classroom's program, but they are not part of the basic provisioning framework for the literacy environment. The literacy environment provides a specialized set of materials visible and available to children as they go about their day; these provisions function in support of a wide variety of learning activities, including but not limited to the spontaneous uses of literacy. Provisions are chosen primarily for their potential support of activity, for their ability to encourage the continuation and display of projects, and for their capacity to highlight connections among ideas, activities, and materials.

The basic provisioning framework is described by six provisioning categories: *raw materials, tools, information sources, containers, work spaces,* and *display facilities.* Each category represents a particular function played by provisions in support of learning activities and contains several types of materials that can fulfill that function in particular ways. The general functions of provisioning categories have been fully described elsewhere (Loughlin & Suina, 1982), so they are reviewed here only briefly.

Raw Materials

Raw materials provide objects and materials children can manipulate, shape, arrange, combine, and recombine in a variety of ways. Both consumable and reusable raw materials are in great demand in the environment, since raw materials are a part of every product that emerges from learning activities. Some raw materials, such as tissue paper or paint, are consumed as they are incorporated into learning activities. Others, like unit blocks or plasticine, can be reused. These provisions serve an important function in the environment because they stimulate ideas and suggest connections among different kinds of materials and influence the products of children's activity. In turn, those products provide a specific focus for literacy activity in which children label, explain, or share information in the displaying of their projects or reporting about their activities.

There are several subcategories of raw materials, some being used in unique ways because of their characteristics, while others have a variety of uses. Construction materials, foods, pigments, and sculpture materials are identified by their adaptability within specific activities, but fabrics, cords, papers, found items, and natural materials are used for a wider range of purposes.

Tools

Tools are all those objects or materials that can be used to process materials or information in some way. Because there are a variety of ways to act on information and materials, a list of items that serve as tools in this framework is much more inclusive than a list of hardware (i.e., paste functions as a joining tool, a crayon as a recording tool, and a temporary insect cage as a viewing tool). Tools shape children's learning activities because they determine what can be done to the materials and information that are used. In a very direct way, tools contribute to learning outcomes and help determine what skills are developed. Fine motor skills are called upon and practiced in the handling of all tools, and academic skills are employed as children use tools for activities such as graphic recording, listening, viewing, or sorting, for example.

Provisions from several groups of tools, including joining tools, viewing tools, cutting and shaping tools, heating and cooling tools, and mixing tools, assist children in all their learning activities. Other types of tools offer special support for particular curriculum areas. Computing tools such as number lines and measuring tools such as rulers are classroom provisions traditionally associated with the mathematics curriculum. Recording tools such as markers are associated with language, and expressing/communicating tools such as puppets are used for the arts. However, even these apparently specialized tools for measuring, computing, recording, or expressing/communicating offer support across a broader range of activities. For instance, children

Basic Provisioning Categories

Raw Materials

Construction materials
Natural materials
Found objects
Fabrics
Cords
Food
Pigments
Papers
Sculpture materials

Containers

Flats
Dry deep
Watertight deep
Cages
Blank books
Racks
Envelopes
Chart papers

Tools

Measuring
Joining
Computing
Cutting and shaping
Mixing
Observing and viewing
Recording
Heating and cooling
Expressing and communicating

Work Spaces

Booths
Mats
Underneaths
Corners
Flat surfaces
Vertical surfaces

Information Sources

References
Communication media
Pictures
Recordings
Natural Specimens
Labels
Books
Models
Charts
Living things

Display Facilities

Bulletin boards
Cases
Shelf space
Stands
Frames
Racks
Label blanks

often use crayons and pencils (recording tools) to label and display their science projects, sometimes employ drama props (expressing/communicating tools) to share knowledge, and at times make use of grid paper or computers (computing tools) to record events symbolically.

Information Sources

Information sources are the materials and objects that provide knowledge content by supplying information children can incorporate into learning activities. Print information sources, like books or reference charts, are traditionally recognized for their information function. Nonprint information sources, such as models and natural specimens, also offer children access to information. Information sources, whether print or nonprint, can offer displayed information as charts or realia do, or they can offer stored information, such as reference books, picture files, or recordings.

Information sources capture children's interest, helping them initiate and remain involved in productive learning, and help determine what ideas or knowledge children encounter, thus shaping the content of children's learning; they also elicit skills related to interpreting and retrieving information.

Books are the most easily identified information sources, but several other forms also support children's ability to obtain information. References and recordings tend to offer stored information requiring some kind of retrieval, but living things, models, natural specimens, realia, labels, and charts display their data. Some media store information and some display it.

Containers

Containers are the objects used by learners to store information, materials, or work-in-progress. Children use containers to arrange and organize information and materials as part of a learning experience, or for later reference and use. Although often considered only as housekeeping materials, this group of provisions can have an important influence on children's learning. Containers encourage depth and complexity in ongoing study by reminding children that projects can be continued beyond the immediately available working time, because they offer the possibility of storage of work-in-progress. Through their function of holding materials or information as children gather and arrange them for a particular activity, containers stimulate planning and preparation.

Containers useful for learning activities are as varied as the materials and kinds of information that will be arranged and stored in them. Flats, watertight deep containers, dry deep containers, cages, envelopes, blank books, chart papers, and racks all support children's ability to extend learning activities in depth or direction.

Work Spaces

Work spaces provide places to work within the environment, either by providing spaces for people, as individuals or in groups, or by providing surfaces to hold materials as the children who use them settle alongside. Variation in work spaces provides appropriate spaces for different kinds of activity, encouraging privacy, cooperative activity, language interaction, and peer support. Work spaces determine the kinds of materials that can be used, since limits on the size of a work space also limit the size of materials that can be accommodated on or within it. Possible movement within learning activities is determined by the amount of space and shelter offered by a work space (Jones & Prescott, 1984), and the capacity of an environment's work spaces to accommodate groups of different sizes influences the potential development of social skills and language.

Adults tend to think mainly of desks and table tops as work spaces, but when children need places to work, others may be more useful. Booths, corners, and underneaths offer places for an individual to be alone, while mats, flat surfaces, and vertical surfaces provide good places to arrange materials. Activity units and undesignated units created by spatial organization and materials arrangement provide spaces for small groups of children to work together.

Display Facilities

Display facilities are the empty spaces and labels children use for the organization and exhibition of materials. This provisioning category refers only to those spaces available to children for use in arranging their own displays. The spaces teachers reserve for instructional display or displays of selected work are not part of this category. Display facilities are designated for temporary occupation only, so children can display their own work and see the work of others. They offer a medium of communication and a sharing of ideas or information, and they also function to stimulate interest in the ideas and projects of others, because one child's display often becomes another child's information source.

Bulletin boards and other arrangements provide for two-dimensional display in an environment, but there is such a variety in the materials and objects children wish to share that other kinds of display facilities are important, too. Frames, shelf space, stands, racks, and cases offer space to present and highlight two- and three-dimensional materials, and blank labels of many sizes and styles support extension of display into child-written titles, explanations, procedures, and sources.

LITERACY CHARACTERISTICS AND PROVISIONS

Provisions play an important role in creating several characteristics of the functioning literacy environment described in chapter 1. Information sources are basic to the literacy environment; they are the major ingredients in *interesting things to read and write about*; and the two characteristics, *references where needed* and *books everywhere*, refer only to information sources. The remaining provisioning categories contribute to the interesting things to read and write about; and they provide *recording tools and materials, varied places to settle down for reading and writing*, and *display spaces and tools*.

Information Sources and Literacy Characteristics

Interesting things to read and write about are essential to a functioning literacy environment, and the majority of these are information sources. Some information sources present information in vivid and concrete form; related symbolic and print forms lead children to extend their information searches once they have become involved. In print and nonprint combinations, information sources seem to beckon children to literacy activity; they begin with interest in the concrete, move toward explorations of symbolic forms of information and on to uses of print in data gathering and recording. A combination of displayed and stored forms of information is also effective because the displayed information, which may or may not be concrete, can generate interest, while stored information sustains the follow-up processes of searching out further and more detailed data.

Variety in information sources has a special relationship to children's literacy activity. Because children are voracious consumers of

Concrete and symbolic information lead to literacy.

information, a lot of information is needed to support the many different directions of inquiry within a group. Children all need access to information that they can use at their own level of development; consequently information is presented in print and nonprint form and at different levels of difficulty.

The more variation there is in the specific materials within an information source category, the greater the learning potential of those provisions will be. Duplicate items offer much less support for literacy growth than the same number of varied provisions because it is the kind and variety of information available rather than the actual number of sources that determine whether the environment's knowledge resources are sufficient.

Books everywhere in the environment encourage children to become enthusiastic about books, because environmental arrangements offer invitations to books at every turn. Displayed books can keep pace with children's activities and interest and reflect community events or relate to seasonal events, and their placement near other provisions highlights those connections. Some books are displayed to invite browsing, others to feature illustrations, and still others to support activities with information or how-to-do-it details. The number is less important than the fit of those books to ongoing events and interests within the environment.

Various publications, child-made and teacher-made books, magazines, directories, and even blank books play important roles in encouraging literacy activity. They are arranged for access in various combinations with tradebooks and individual textbooks, with nonprint information sources, and with materials from other provisioning categories.

Nonprint information sources combined with books can clarify the meaning of the print by providing a visible and often concrete context for it.

References where they are needed are important as they are information sources that contain specialized information, sometimes in list or outline form and sometimes in brief narratives. Often, the information is organized so a user can find it rapidly. When the literacy environment is in full operation, children display a hunger for information that gives immediate help with their learning activities and for information that makes connections with the ideas and topics currently engaging their interest and efforts. It is helpful if they can locate that information independently and easily.

In addition to the conventional reference books, children make references of word lists, parts of trade books (index, table of contents), diagrams of maps, pictures, alphabet cards, and calendars. When they become involved with interesting content, children's needs for information broaden, and more comprehensive references, like an encyclopedia or nonfiction trade books, become important as they search for information.

As children become familiar with print conventions, the demand for related references increases. Beginning writers look for words and models in the environment as they write; older children may seek references in composing and the proofreading process.

Contributions of Other Provisioning Categories

Some tools function in the same way as the interesting things to read and write about that focus children's literacy activities.

Variety rather than duplication is emphasized in the choice of tools. Different tools for different functions, such as joining, cutting and shaping, or computing, help children recognize interesting and intriguing attributes of their materials. A choice of tools allows different ways of approaching any project, so children need more information guiding their choice of tools, and they need accurate terminology to discuss their choices and label their displays. This often leads them to references and other print information sources, contributing to vocabulary growth and a respect for precision and specificity in language about the function of tools.

Raw materials extend the environment's interesting things to read and write about, too. They may suggest one book-binding process rather than another, depending on texture or thickness or some other attribute. Children sometimes become interested in how a book can be physically constructed from a particular raw material and then become involved with writing, because their concept of a book tells them that the pages should contain words or illustrations. At other times, these materials may stimulate writing because they suggest a product that represents some personal experience or interesting idea. However, raw materials stimulate much more than making and binding books. Variety in the materials supports individually designed products as outcomes of learning activities. Raw materials are used in most learning activities and can instigate particular projects or products. They offer purposes for literacy when children make preparations by researching, planning, and diagraming, or listing materials needed. Whether or not they contain print, products that children design provide much more motivation for written explanation and display than products designed by teachers but executed by children.

In a less direct way, containers also help extend the amount of interesting things for children to read and write about. Containers large enough to hold an assortment of materials gathered for an activity can prompt planning ahead, with the literacy activities that may be associated with planning. The presence of containers also suggests that there is time to continue an interesting project over more than one day; this, in turn, increases the probability that literacy will be involved, since information seeking is part of extended inquiry.

Recording tools and materials everywhere in the literacy environment are constant reminders that information, ideas, and events can be recorded in print and in other symbolic forms that are also part of literacy. It is easy to see that writing tools are needed for the production of print because their presence and location in the environment determine whether or not children become spontaneously involved with writing. However, there are other tools that also serve recording functions, and planned variety in these offer a range of forms that provide unique and varied experiences for individuals and keep interest in recording high.

Potential support for practice is closely related to the variety of recording tools provided for children's access, because different tools elicit different skills. Even a collection of recording tools limited to pens can broaden the fine motor skills of handwriting such as control of line, pressure, ink flow, hand movements, and spacing as children adapt to the characteristics of ball-point, calligraphy, felt-tipped, fine-point, broad-point, indelible, and fountain pens. The range of skills expands further when the variety of recording tools includes pencils, a tape recorder, chalk, paintbrushes, printing stamps or a printing press, letter stencils, a typewriter, magnetic letters, or a word-processing computer program.

The recording materials that are so important in stimulating children to spontaneous writing are, of course, raw materials. Raw materials are essential for symbolic representation, in two- and three-dimensional forms, as children represent information through models, pictures, diagrams, tallies, or graphs, and they are also necessary for the preparation of all print materials. The shapes, sizes, textures, and colors of available paper make a difference in what children do with it. Long, narrow paper may promote list making; large-sized paper seems to stimulate written public announcements; short, wide strips generate captions or titles; stationery and postcard-sized paper accompanied by some kind of stickers get children involved in personal communications for mailboxes; and small pads suggest note taking. In addition to these direct influences on children's literacy, variety in raw materials has strong indirect effects. Stiff papers of variegated colors encourage mounting and labeling of two-dimensional materials for display, at-

Shapes and sizes of paper influence their use.

tractively colored and differently textured papers create interest in special bindings for books, and varied papers for drawing, painting, and collage encourage children to make illustrations of their compositions. Blank books stimulate literacy, as children label the pictures of other two-dimensional materials placed in them.

Places to settle down for reading and writing seem to be an obvious need for any school setting. It is easy to overlook the importance of work spaces as a necessary component of the literacy environment, but they are a strong support to literacy. Without a variety of work spaces there is relatively little spontaneous literacy activity, because literacy occurs within a social context of sharing and communication and is a part of many situations and social settings.

For children literacy is often more of a social activity than a solitary one. The social aspect of books, including showing pictures, pointing out things, reading aloud, or comparing the books, is important (Collins, 1984). So is the social aspect of composition, as children rehearse their writing by talking about it, read aloud a newly constructed sentence, or discuss the best way to spell something. An

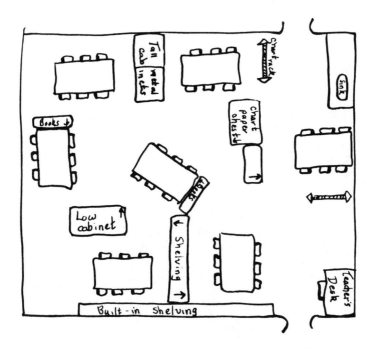

Work spaces for groups encourage shared literacy.

environment that provides settings for small groups to talk together, read to one another, or share personal writing in the long run stimulates more individual literacy than an environment with only quiet, individual work spaces.

The *display spaces and tools* that support children as they share their products and messages are a complete provisioning category. Although no single category functions alone in its influence on literacy behaviors, children's display facilities frequently offer children the first and strongest reason for writing and provide a powerful stimulus for reading what others have written. Over time the opportunity to display one's work and to claim it publicly with a signature grows into a pattern of sharing information and commentary and responding in print to the displays of classmates.

The proportion of visible print that is child-generated is a good indicator of a literacy environment's ability to function well, making the use of literacy a way of life in the classroom, but this cannot occur without many places available to children for their own arrangements of materials. Many display facilities keep children's participation in the production of the environment's literacy at a high level, giving them a reason to write and at the same time offering interesting content in the form of shared print messages and information. Display facilities stimulate the sharing of products and ideas, further increasing the potential content of literacy as children prepare materials for others to see and read.

THE HOLDING POWER OF PROVISIONS

Some provisions readily attract and hold interest, keeping children involved in learning activities for fairly long periods of time, and that

Display facilities offer strong motivation for writing.

holding power comes from several different characteristics of the materials. Children are especially interested in provisions reflecting their homes and community (Loughlin & Suina, 1983); those special qualities make children feel familiar and comfortable. The adaptability of provisions to different settings enables children to stay with them through several different activities, and complexity in learning materials offers different kinds of actions and uses within a single activity (Kritchevsky, Prescott, & Walling, 1977). Adaptability and complexity increase the likelihood that children will encounter the potential learning opportunities the provisions offer.

Community Reflections

For many children there is a great contrast between the world as they know it at home and the world they encounter in school. The differences are most marked when there is cultural distance between learning in the community and learning in the school. When a teacher adds materials from the community's natural environment, from children's homes, and from other local sources, the environment begins to resemble the community, offering a message of welcome and acceptance, influencing children's feelings of comfort and their attitudes as they approach learning materials. Community-connected materials offer holding power and provide a stimulus for literacy, whether or not they include print. They provide a very personal context for literacy by reflecting children's real lives, encouraging children to share and celebrate community life, and helping them connect the learning that occurs in the school setting with what they learn in the community.

Community materials create familiar contexts.

Multiuse Materials

Multiuse materials lend themselves to many different settings and combinations because they can be acted upon with a variety of tools and processes. Aggregate materials such as sand, materials that have a permanent form such as found objects, and other raw materials can add complexity to provisioned areas. Certain basic tools for recording, viewing, or measuring are used in different ways in different settings, and their multiple possibilities for use encourage extension of activity to new actions and processes, increasing the holding power of each area. Children often take multiuse materials from one activity into another, remaining involved with the provisions as the activities change.

Complexity

Complex materials have holding power because they present many possibilities for action. Most of the environment's complexity comes from combinations of materials, but there are differences in the amount of complexity offered by specific materials, too. Some materials (i.e., mechanical construction kits) are complex because they have subparts that can be used in different ways, others (i.e., puppets) because they are materials that encourage improvising, and some (i.e., classroom pets) because they present a certain amount of unpredictability. On the other hand, simple materials (i.e., puzzles, lotto games) offer only a single activity possibility. When an environment has a predominance of simple materials, it's difficult for children to maintain involvement for long periods because there are few choices for action, so there isn't much chance that they will work in depth. Complexity in provisioning helps children develop and maintain commitment to their work and increases the likelihood that they will extend their activities into literacy.

3

Materials Arrangement and Literacy

Making decisions about the *distribution* of provisions is an important part of the teacher's environmental role during the establishment of the literacy environment. Teachers' initial decisions about materials distribution are connected to spatial organization, implying some particular arrangement of the furniture designated to hold the provisions used in children's learning activities. Teachers also make daily decisions about materials distribution as part of their work behind the scenes when they add, change, or reorganize materials in the environment. These daily decisions are concerned with the distribution of materials to stimulate activities involving symbols and print wherever children may be.

Somewhat different decisions about materials arrangement are concerned with the *display* of materials for visual and physical access. The appearance of materials is determined by the holders and organizers used for display and by the ways the specific materials are arranged within them. These features of materials display have great influence on children's awareness of the materials, on apparent material preferences, and on the particular uses made of available provisions (Loughlin & Suina, 1982). Arrangements are carefully designed to highlight the appearance of provisions and provide physical access at the same time.

THE ALPHABET

A seven-year-old in Mrs. Lee's classroom was working very hard at writing something that seemed important to him. He moved close to the chalkboard beneath which a set of colorful cartoon-decorated alphabet cards were lined up. Frequently he frowned, looking from his paper to the cards and back again. From time

35

to time he went over to the cards and moved along them, putting his index finger directly on a letter or sometimes moving along the chart as if searching. He was serious and persistent in his work and finally finished his writing.

Later that day when the children were in a group meeting, the teacher asked if there was any new business. "Yes!" said Tony. "Will you *please* straighten up the alphabet?" Because Mrs. Lee had very carefully lined up the alphabet cards under the chalkboard, she was puzzled.

"It *is* straight!" several children retorted.

"No it *isn't!* Look!" argued Tony, and he went to the cards, pointing to the letters themselves, which were in varied placement on the cards: some on top, some in the middle, some at the lower edge. Each individual card was designed for attractive balance between vivid illustration and letter, so that in the alphabet as a whole the letters were not in a straight line at all. Each letter had to be searched for in its eccentric artistic arrangement.

Mrs. Lee was puzzled at first that only one child was aware that the letters were not uniformly placed on the cards. Why hadn't the other children noticed that, or at least seen it when Tony asked her to "straighten up the alphabet"? Then she realized that only Tony was still unsure of the shape of letters and needed to use the cards as a reference. Locating the shapes he needed from all of the figures on the cards was difficult enough, because the busy background tended to camouflage the letters. The uneven letter placement added to the effort of visually locating the needed model.

A day or two later Mrs. Lee located a more traditional set of manuscript alphabet cards, showing clear upper- and lower-case letters on guide lines against a plain green background. She put the decorated alphabet above the chalkboard to be enjoyed as art work and placed the new cards under the chalkboard where Tony could see them easily.

The teacher reflected on the differences between the way she and Tony perceived the illustrated alphabet cards and wondered why she hadn't realized Tony was having difficulty. She frequently checked the environment's appearance from the children's eye level and tried to display materials so they were visually clear, but she hadn't noticed how confusing the alphabet cards could be. Finally she concluded that for Tony, as a beginner, it was necessary that the total outline of the letters be visible, so he could see them. However, like most literate adults, she had thoroughly internalized letter configuration, so she could "see" individual letters with very little visual information. She had been unable to see the alphabet in the same way Tony did, until he pointed it out to her.

DISTRIBUTION OF MATERIALS

When the environment is first set up, a pattern for the distribution of learning materials is established and tends to remain consistent over time. It may be a pattern of centralized storage, with all similar provisions such as the pencils, the scissors, or the library books kept together, or it may be a decentralized pattern, with similar materials separated and placed in many locations around the environment. Distribution determines when and where children encounter provisions related to literacy, making distribution an important influence on how materials are put to use in learning activities, or whether they are used at all.

A centralized pattern, in which materials are stored together because they are similar, is associated with fairly short involvement with any activity, due to interruptions as children travel to storage units for needed tools and materials. Children often have difficulty in initiating activities or elaborating them to incorporate literacy when centralized storage is used because the materials that could have suggested those actions are carefully stored with others of their kind, away from children's work areas.

Decentralized patterns, locating materials on the basis of their role in stimulating learning rather than on the basis of their similarity, are associated with longer involvement in learning activities, with self-direction, and with persistence. Decentralizing materials releases provisions from single-category storage so that different provisioning categories can be combined in a variety of ways to stimulate a wide range of activities and to associate literacy with those activities.

Centralized Storage and Literacy Activity

Centralized materials storage tends to create problems for the functioning literacy environment because the materials most likely to be stored by category are recording tools and materials, references, library books, and other print and nonprint information sources. When these literacy-related materials are stored by category, often they are out of sight, except for those persons working close to the storage area. The old adage "Out of sight, out of mind" is a good description of the problem that is created, because children tend to make independent use of only the tools and materials clearly visible, in or near the places where they are working. Recording tools at the back of the classroom, paper in the closet, library books behind the screen, and interesting nonprint information sources stored at the edges of the environment, away from work spaces or pathways, remain unnoticed and unused, unless children are directed to them by the teacher. Stored-away materials aren't available to stimulate the spontaneous use of literacy.

In some settings, where teachers have moved toward a literacy environment to the point of displaying a considerable amount of print, hoping to interest children in its messages and invite them to respond in some way, it seems puzzling when children don't appear to attend to those invitations. But if materials are arranged in single-category storage, the stimulus and the means for response are separated, so the impulse to make use of literacy is not supported. When this happens it's easy to think that children are uninterested or haven't adequate ability to make use of literacy.

Decentralizing Literacy Materials

Reorganizing literacy materials from centralized storage is more than just doing away with a single storage cabinet where all the supplies are kept. It begins with examining provisions, considering how each can contribute to a context for literacy, and how they can encourage children to initiate daily uses of literacy. Applying a basic principle of materials arrangement, that the placement of materials side by side strongly suggests their combination (Kritchevsky, Prescott,

Children use provisions
near their work spaces.

& Walling, 1977) and implies connections among them, teachers place materials where possibilities for their use exist. In places where literacy is not suggested they may place a note pad and pencils beside a reference to suggest note taking, or put paper and felt pens near a balance scale to suggest making records of procedures or findings.

The distribution of materials in small quantities in several locations stimulates literacy related to the activities involving other provisions in the area. In most literacy environments, holders containing a small number of common tools and materials for literacy are arranged with or near all other provisions. Two or three pencils, markers, and crayons, with recording materials such as pads or typing paper, some word lists and a dictionary for references, and a few joining and display tools in each collection are often enough to remind children to report, record, display, or make notes about their activities. Adding one or two content-relevant books, print references, photographs, diagrams, or other nonprint information sources also related to the basic materials of the area extends literacy potential still further. Additional trade books, references, and other information sources are placed throughout the environment to function in the same way.

Teachers in functioning literacy environments seem to place literacy stimuli in all the areas, including some not commonly considered in connection with growth in literacy. Art materials, blocks, number rods, playground equipment, photo albums, window sill plants, sand tables, nature study collections, calculators, newspaper clippings, and any other imaginable information sources or materials collections seem to function as natural starting places for the uses of literacy. An involvement with these materials leads to an involvement with literacy when they are arranged with the appropriate literacy provisions. Literacy materials make their own strong suggestions because of their placement in a particular area. Wherever there is a stimulus for literacy, there is also, in the same place, a means for response to that stimulus (Ivener, 1983).

In addition to the powerful suggestions for literacy that are created by a decentralized placement of materials, these arrangements also affect children's physical access to materials, which in turn affects their use. The distribution of materials offers better physical access than keeping them clustered together because it minimizes the crowding or traffic congestion that occurs in limited space when many individuals attempt to get to materials in the same display at the same time. With the congestion that comes from centrally organized materials, some children can easily get to materials, but others will be left without or will have to be extremely persistent to obtain access.

Distributing Display Facilities

In the functioning literacy environment, there is an important reason for applying the principles of materials arrangement to children's display spaces and tools. Display facilities are the empty spaces and labels available to children for arranging their own displays. Their function is to provide useful communication in the learning environment, stimulating interest in the ideas and projects of classmates while providing context and encouragement for literacy, as children prepare and label their own displays and examine the displays of classmates. One child's display becomes another child's stimulus for activity and for the use of literacy connected with that activity.

A functioning literacy environment provides different kinds of display spaces in all areas, so that children's print and other works can be placed where it will be seen and where it can be related to other materials nearby. Backs and sides of shelf units are pressed into service as display spaces; so are spaces low on the wall that can be seen by children seated in an area, although they may not catch an adult's eye. Dividers or bookcases, empty desk surfaces, doors, and a variety of racks and stands also can display children's materials well.

When some display space is available in every area, environments present a good deal of spontaneous writing, which in turn stimulates further uses of reading and recording. When each area contains a

Children display work in all areas.

collection of common literacy materials, display space, and display tools arranged for children's access, child-generated written material is found in generous quantities (Sheehan & Cole, 1983).

DISPLAYING LITERACY MATERIALS

The legibility of displayed print is created in part by the form of the print itself; equally important, however, is the way it is displayed. Children not yet completely secure with letter forms and other conventions of print are helped in their attempts to gain meaning from print when it is displayed with visual clarity. Children already reading are most likely to be aware of print and its messages when careful display provides legibility, highlights the content of print, and at the same time calls attention to other provisions for literacy. Arrangements that produce effective display also support children's production.

Display for Visibility

In order for print to be legible, it must first be visible from the spaces children use when working or moving through the environment. Displayed print is visible and remains that way when it is posted without overlapping materials and when furniture and other stacked and stored materials do not conceal it from potential readers. Print placed at or below the eye level of children is more useful in classrooms than print above eye level, which is not often used except by assignment or when a teacher directs children's attention to it for some specific purpose. Because of the differences in adults' and children's views of the learning environment, the best way to see whether print is visible is to move down to children's eye level at standing and sitting height and scan the environment from all the spaces children use for work or traffic (Loughlin, 1977).

Even clear and unobstructed print may not be visible to its intended audience if it is placed where the children rarely go. Print can be highly visible on the walls, the backs or sides of cabinets, or on dividers and chart racks within activity areas where children settle down for work; on dividers or furniture that define the pathways used to move from place to place; or at the central display places where everybody looks for important daily information.

The potential uses of tools and materials for literacy require those materials be clearly visible, too. Recording tools, such as pencils, markers and other pens, colored pencils, or crayons, are most used when they are clearly visible in an uncovered holder, within physical reach. Writing paper and other recording materials are seen and used when they are spread out rather than stacked and when different types of paper, lined or unlined, for example, or with different textures or colors, are presented with enough space showing so children can quickly identify their characteristics. Children select more varied recording materials when they can take one piece without dropping or shifting several others, and without rummaging through a pile of materials in order to find a suitable one.

Open holders stimulate the spontaneous uses of literacy because they show their contents clearly. Depending upon vertical placement, sides may be transparent when materials are right at eye level, or solid when materials are on low shelves with contents visible from above. The holders may have open sides, fronts, tops, or partially open sections that leave materials visible. The best holder for any set of materials is determined by the particular materials or collection to be displayed. Deep holders can hold and display some recording tools upright, but most recording materials are better seen and reached in relatively shallow holders.

Decorated Print

Sometimes the print displayed in a learning environment looks attractive to adults but is not perceptually clear to the children who need to make use of it. The decorations are not really the information children need when referring to print, yet they may be the dominant

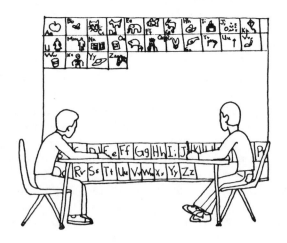

Useful print is undecorated and displayed at eye level.

feature of a display. When decorations produce more visual stimuli than letter forms, they tend to camouflage print, or at the very least, they make it necessary for children to search beneath all that busy design for the print—a difficult task.

Background for Display

The background upon which materials are displayed can either clarify those materials or camouflage them. Plain, undecorated backgrounds offer no competing stimuli to confuse the eye and muddle the information needed to clearly perceive the displayed materials. Print is easily overpowered by a patterned background, making reading difficult. Clearly contrasting colors or textures, especially when the colors are deep and clear and the textures subdued in pattern, can show displayed materials without overwhelming them (Loughlin, 1982).

The same effects hold true for the appearance of other provisions in the environment. Markers, pencils, and scissors in open but decorated holders sometimes remain unused because they aren't clearly seen

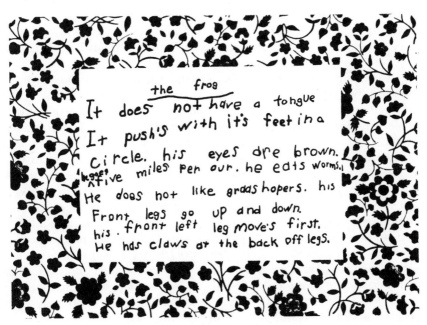

the frog
It does not have a tongue
It push's with it's feet in a
circle. his eyes are brown.
he at five miles per our. he eats worms.
He does not like grasshopers. his
Front legs go up and down.
his front left leg moves first.
He has claws at the back off legs.

Print is easily overpowered.

within the holders. When old shelving is spruced up with shelf paper to make the environment more attractive, the particular shelf paper that is selected has crucial effects on the appearance of the materials placed there. If that shelf paper is covered with a pattern, the designs can overcome the visibility of the materials in the open holders. On the other hand, plain-colored shelf paper, in deep, clear tones that highlight the materials in their holders, can increase children's awareness and use of them.

Highlighting Materials by Display

Clear display of literacy provisions and of print calls for some control in the quantity of displayed materials. When there is an array of materials in one location, it is sometimes difficult to identify the individual items within the array. In order to clarify the display, related materials are grouped together, then those groups are separated a bit, then each group is surrounded with empty space. Occasionally this requires reducing the quantity of some materials; however, with each step, the visual focus on the materials becomes stronger, and the print or provisions become more noticeable.

Decentralized material arrangements make it easier to control the quantity of displayed materials, because decentralizing calls for subdividing supplies into smaller sets in a number of different locations. Small quantities of displayed provisions can be replenished at regular intervals from stored supplies.

It is equally important to control the quantity of displayed print, because the larger the empty space surrounding a print segment, the more attention will focus on the print and the greater its legibility. This calls for rotation of posted written materials so that display is short term, and replacement of one item with another happens on a daily basis. Materials are highlighted when they are seen within an enclosing form that frames them and strongly directs the eye to the display within the form. In print display this is accomplished with backing or framing. Holders often create the enclosing forms for materials display, and sometimes a waiting placemat or tape-marked section of a shelf frames the place to which the holder is returned.

Clearly displayed materials are most likely to capture attention when they are placed in areas where they will be seen and noticed as children glance about and move from place to place. New materials or print are highlighted when displayed with provisions that already hold high interest and are connected in some way with the new materials.

Provisions well displayed for children's access are most used when arranged within arms' reach, close enough for touching and handling. Generally, arrangements that provide visual clarity also provide good physical access, if space is organized to enable children to get to the shelving or display area where materials are displayed.

Highlighting Displayed Print

Teacher's Display
Post at eye level or below
Keep background plain, undecorated
Surround print segments with empty
  space
Place print within an enclosing form
Control quantity displayed
Keep print current

Children's Display
Prepare oversized backing for beginners
Mark spaces for print with outlines or
  backing
Encourage dating of displays
Organize short-term rotating display

Helping Children Display Print

Most of the print in functioning literacy environments is produced and displayed by children. The opportunity to display their products increases children's interest in written expression and communication, so the quantity of print generated by children implies that much of the display is theirs. Environmental arrangements help children display print well, making sure it is readable so others can attend to its message.

As children display their own writings, they place them at their own eye level or lower, and this meets one criteria for effective display. Because display space above eye level isn't very usable for children, some teachers share large-sized bulletin boards, leaving the lower sections for children's display and using the upper levels for teacher display. Children are comfortable arranging and reading displayed print on walls or cabinets fairly close to the floor, where it will be seen by those who settle nearby.

When children's writing is inexpert, its legibility can be enhanced by enlarging the empty area around the print. It's easier for children to do this when designated display spaces for single items are already marked by large pieces of solid colored paper or framing outlines of various proportions. Established boundaries help keep the surrounding spaces empty, and children can be encouraged to write on paper to fit a given space by the placement of that paper close to the designated space. Arranging a few sheets of oversized backing paper beside the display space is another way to encourage children to arrange a display clearly.

The sizes of displayed print segments in any environment vary, depending on their functions, from short announcements, captions, or queries to informational reports or stories. There are sometimes reasons to encourage special locations for special kinds of writing, and to some extent the sizes of display spaces affect children's preferred locations for particular kinds of writing. Children tend to locate the display materials they need, then to use available posting places near those materials, so the sizes and kinds of backing and labeling materials in an area also influence where children go to display particular writings.

For some children, aligning displayed materials may be difficult without assistance. Lining up the print segment may not be very important for some messages briefly displayed for a small audience, but generally print materials are clearer when the print itself is level. Precut backing fastened to display surfaces is helpful, and in some literacy environments a string line is used to keep display straight. Permanently located tacks at measured intervals on each side of a bulletin board hold string level while the material is being posted, and the string is removed easily after the display is arranged.

Keeping Print Current

Planning is required to ensure that print remains current, but it is important. In functioning literacy environments it's not just the presence of print that matters, but the meaning of that print. Old print just consumes display space without offering any new information. After all, how important can the meaning of yesterday's schedule be? Display space is at a premium; yet clear display requires empty space surrounding each print segment, so it limits the amount of material that can be displayed at any given time. When the environment functions well to stimulate uses of literacy, large quantities of print are produced by children and teachers, and the print needs to be displayed with some control of quantity. Keeping the displayed print current is one way, because it establishes a time limit to most display. A child who doesn't find enough display space knows that some will be available later, and the print in the environment remains fresh and informative. Over time a large amount of print can be displayed and will be read, though the quantity is limited on any particular day.

The number of days that a particular segment of displayed print remains current depends on its function. When the time frame has been established, the age of the display is made public by accurate dating so everyone knows which writings can be removed and which stay. Calendars are located in all areas of the environment to encourage this.

Often children want to save materials they have displayed, so they remove their own, but someone else may remove outdated print when its writer isn't immediately available. Special containers in an area, reserved for print that has been removed from display, may help keep peace in environments where children are excited about their writings and want to retrieve them. When a person's print display has been taken down by someone else, it will be easy to find and retrieve it later. And meantime, something new and interesting to read has appeared in its place.

DIFFERENT KINDS OF PRINT DISPLAY

Arranging print in the functioning literacy environment calls for some special considerations, reflecting the need to control the quantity of print in order to keep it legible and reflecting the purpose or audience for that print.

There are three major reasons for displaying the written word in the learning environment. One of these is to provide opportunities for children to read symbols and print. This requires *readable display*, which must be perceptually clear so children can easily see and distinguish elements of writing. The principles of effective display are applied to the display of readable print, so the messages of the print are always emphasized and so everybody has access to them. Materials intended for readable display are of interest when posted in all areas where learning activities occur, and some are useful in a central location. Most of the print teachers place in the environment is intended for readable display, and much of the print that children contribute is too.

Another reason to display print is to develop awareness of writing as a medium for reflection, expression, and pleasure. This calls for a large quantity of written materials in *appreciative display* for others to know about and enjoy; this display tells children that their writing is appreciated and displayed. Appreciative display is arranged in different places from readable display. Arrangements that are like galleries, displaying a larger number of items than would ordinarily appear in readable display, are very useful. Reserving these display spaces for appreciative display helps clarify the nature of the print displayed there and also invites browsing. Spaces children pass through, but don't stay in, make good locations for appreciative display. Tack strips near coat closets and doorways, above chalkboards, and along heavily traveled pathways display these materials well. When teachers and children from several literacy environments share a common entry or hallway, appreciative display is sometimes arranged in those spaces. It's very likely that some of the writings in appreciative display will not be read by all, but the writers know their work is appreciated, and can direct readers to it.

Sometimes materials for appreciative display are arranged in packages, such as collected works gathered in book form or in special folders of related writings of different authors. When the collections are displayed within physical reach, children have easy access to them, and they will be more legible than in overcrowded single-item displays.

Different Kinds of Print Display

Readable Display
  Provides opportunites for children to
    read symbols and print
  Perceptually clear arrangements

Appreciative Display
  Focuses on awareness of writing as a
    medium for reflection, expression,
    and pleasure
  Gallery arrangements
  Larger arrangements

Visitor Display
  Offers information to parents, guests
  Posted at adult eye level
  Quantity determined by amount of
    information

For *visitor display* still different arrangements of print offer particular information about program, schedule, and other classroom events for parents and other guests interested in what is happening in the environment. Because the audience for visitor display is usually adult, this print can be posted effectively in places that are usually out of the children's vision range. Bulletin board space above children's eye level, wall space above a teacher's desk, and higher spaces close to the entry into the environment are good places for visitor display.

Although some teachers prefer to locate visitor display just outside the door, rather than give up display space within the environment, others find advantages in placing some inside, in areas that would not be effective for readable display intended for children. Current visitor display invites the visitors to read the posted information, and as they read they provide models of adults reading for information, providing yet another stimulus for children's daily uses of literacy.

4

Spatial Organization and Literacy

Observations of environments in which children are actively engaged with literacy throughout the day show some common patterns of room arrangement (Loughlin & Ivener, 1984, February) and reveal the strong, if indirect, role of spatial organization in the support of literacy. In high-literacy classrooms, bookshelves and cabinets are moved away from the edges of the room, and space is divided into clearly defined areas. Seating furniture is dispersed, rather than arranged in a single area, and tables or desk groups are close to materials storage. Such patterns of spatial organization support literacy by interacting with the environment's provisioning and materials arrangement; in addition, they influence children's activity and movement. Effective spatial organization for literacy enables children to function successfully in all learning activities by supporting efforts to meet the demands and behavior expectations of programs and teachers.

Each time a piece of furniture is put into place, spaces are defined, and children's perceptions of those spaces influence their apparent interests, their contact with materials, and their ability to sustain involvement with learning experiences. The extensive information available about spatial organization and its effects on classroom events offers guidance for all aspects of classroom arrangement (Loughlin & Suina, 1982), but this discussion focuses only on spatial organization in relation to the special purposes of the literacy environment.

THE NONREADING CLASSROOM

Several weeks into the school year, Mr. Zamora couldn't see why the fifth graders weren't reading when they had such a wonderful classroom library. It was almost necessary to place books in their hands to get them involved, although most seemed to enjoy reading, once they began.

He was thinking about this before school one morning as he looked over the classroom books to prepare for a new social studies unit. He noticed again how well the large collection represented the current interests of the group. The books were carefully grouped and lined up, spines out, on two tall shelf units that stood against the walls in the library corner at the back of the room. They were topically grouped, with labels on the shelf edges so readers could locate books by subject. A round table in front of the bookcases provided a reading place, or children could carry books to other locations if they preferred. Mr. Zamora could see the entire library clearly from any place in the room, and he just couldn't understand why the children didn't use the books more.

After the children arrived, Mr. Zamora sat down in an unoccupied student chair for a moment to sign something, and as he glanced across the room to see who was in the library, he was surprised to discover that only the topmost shelves were visible. All other books had disappeared from view. When he checked the view of the library books from student chairs in several places, it became clear that they couldn't be seen from most of the work spaces. Many of the chairs placed children with their backs to the library, so they saw no books at all. Even in places where chairs faced the library, children were more apt to see the furnishings of the reading circle than the library, because the furnishings blocked the view of the lower library shelves. From other locations, anybody who looked from the children's eye level still saw only the library's round table and its chairs, which concealed most of the books behind it. The teacher began then to watch the children to see who *did* use a book now and then and saw that everyone who picked up a library book was at a work space close to the library at the time, while those working in other parts of the environment made no use of the books.

It seemed important to get the books closer to the children at each work space, so Mr. Zamora began to plan ways to rearrange the library shelf units. The two library bookshelves were in the same corner of the room, so furniture rearrangement was needed to get some of the books out of the corner. Those shelf units seemed too tall to be placed in the center of the room, although books displayed on the shelves would certainly be visible there, so Mr. Zamora left them near the walls but put them in different parts of the room, placing their narrow ends against the wall, allowing access to both sides of the open shelves. Now book space was available in more than one location, and books were now visible from several directions, and the same rearrangement created sheltered spaces on both sides of each shelf unit.

The library books were reshelved in the new locations, arranged face out so the covers were visible, but now they couldn't all fit in the original shelf space. Thinking that children would be most aware of the books displayed close to work spaces, Mr. Zamora moved two low shelf units away from the walls to the center of the room where they could hold books and other provisions near the students. Now books were within view and reach of everybody, and the new arrangement also created better traffic patterns that helped children get to the books without disturbing others.

After these changes, children began to show more interest in reading. Every time he scanned the classroom, Mr. Zamora saw several children with books, and he noticed individuals making a variety of choices. In addition to choosing from the books placed close to them, children began to go to other areas to make selections. It seemed that the books nearby also reminded the children of books elsewhere and prompted them to seek those books. At

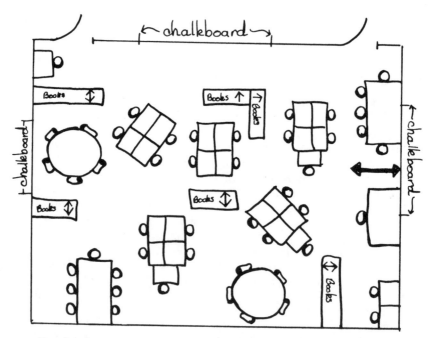

Books for everybody were within view and reachable.

the same time, the paths defined by the placement of shelf units made it possible for children to get to the books easily. The natural interest in books the teacher had expected to see in the children was evident, now that it was supported and extended by environmental arrangements.

EFFECTS OF SPATIAL ORGANIZATION

Spatial organization can support literacy activity in several ways. Furniture placement defines areas that can shelter an individual or group from interruption and intrusion and at the same time creates the paths used to gain physical access to literacy materials and displayed print. Visual access to displayed literacy can be enhanced through spatial organization, too, provided it is planned with a child's eye view in mind. Arrangements of space can contribute to provisioning by establishing some of the environment's work spaces and display facilities, and also to materials arrangement through the location of furniture that can hold displayed materials. Because of the influence of spatial messages on children's behavior, children can be encouraged to notice, approach, and make use of displayed literacy materials and messages through carefully planned organization of space.

Shelter for Literacy Activity

Furniture arrangement, defining spaces within the environment, creates *units* (Kritchevsky, Prescott, & Walling, 1977), the specific spaces children can enter and settle in for learning activities. Units established within an environment provide places for individuals and small groups to move away from all the other events and activities that are going on and to contain their own activity so they don't intrude on others. Furniture placement and the organization of units occur together, and the overall patterns of furniture arrangement determine the amount of shelter that can be established. For instance, if all the shelving, dividers, display screens, book racks, and other space-dividing furniture line the walls, the arrangement defines only one large space for children's activity. Everybody in the environment, with all their activities and all their materials, is located in that one space, and the arrangement offers no separation of one activity from another or one group from another. With no shelter from intrusion, children in such environments are quite distractible and dependent on adult supervision and direction.

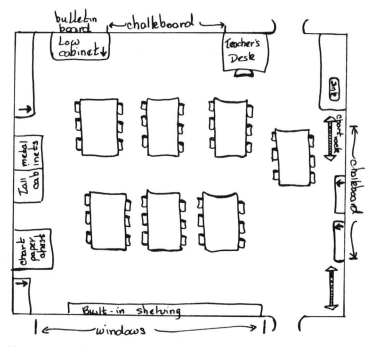

If shelving lines the wall, the room is one big space.

On the other hand, if space-dividing furniture is moved away from the edge of a room and arranged to provide several space divisions and define paths for movement, those units offer a variety of places to work, enabling children to sustain their focus and involvement because they are separated from other ongoing activities. Better work focus and less need for supervision result from this type of spatial organization.

A unit offers shelter from interruption and intrusion, depending on its location, its size, and how its boundaries are defined (Jones & Prescott, 1984). Units can be described in terms of shelter provided, as partially screened units (with one- or two-sided protection), insulated units (at least three-sided protection and room for three or four children), or individual hide units (small, enclosed spaces for one or two children). It is mainly the physical boundaries along the edges of a unit that affect the amount of intrusion that may occur, although sometimes size and location may also affect this. For instance, larger insulated units in which several children are recording experimental data may attract the interest of others, who approach or linger in the vicinity of the activity, and those in units located close to high-density traffic areas or near units with a high level of physical activity may be very aware of the movement or sounds nearby.

Before a space has been provisioned, it is a *potential unit*, but when materials are provided for children's activities, it is an *activity unit*. When children begin to make use of the materials in an activity unit, there is always some physical movement involved. It may be rather contained activity (like reaching for a book, getting out of a chair, or moving across the unit to hang a display) or it might be more active movements, such as acting out charades and role playing or constructing with large-scale materials. As children become involved in learning activity, their physical actions use space that extends beyond the furniture making up the unit, and this *surrounding space* (Kritchevsky, Prescott, & Walling, 1977) functions as part of the unit. When spatial organization preserves the appropriate surrounding space needed for each unit, it provides sufficient room for activity and also acts as a buffer between units or pathways, or between neighboring units, to shelter children from distraction. On the other hand, overlapping of the surrounding space of neighboring units is one of the most common causes for restlessness, limited attention, and a lack of the sustained involvement that is necessary for children to extend their learning activities into literacy, because children in each unit bump into, or are distracted by, children working in the next unit whenever any physical movement is necessary.

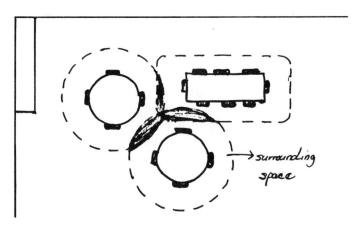

Overlapping surrounding space creates distractions.

Spatial Organization and Access

In addition to organizing spaces for learning activity, furniture arrangement creates paths. Paths are broad, elongated spaces people use to move from place to place; to function appropriately paths must remain empty. This means spaces used for paths aren't available to become parts of units or their surrounding space. People use paths only if they can see them clearly from their own eye level, and they use any path most when something interesting at the far end makes the path an approach to inviting areas or materials.

Careful arrangement of paths leading to activity units provisioned for literacy gives children physical access to the print, tools, and other displayed materials that can stimulate literacy activity. The paths are defined by the backs and sides of furniture that also provide shelter in the insulated and partially screened units where children work. Used this way, shelving furniture sets a boundary of an activity unit and defines a path at the same time. This is more effective than placing the furniture beneath a wall-hung bulletin board at the end of the path, because there it can block children from physically reaching the displays that attracted them in the first place.

In kindergarten and early primary classrooms low furniture, like two-shelf bookcases or low dividers, can function as walls and keep children from gaining the overview of the total environment that the teacher has. The paths visible from adult eye level often disappear when viewed from children's sitting height, unless they were originally arranged and verified from children's eye level. Paths that children see clearly give them access to areas and materials for literacy activity and provide space for the movement and accompanying conversation that is part of a day's work, while sheltering those working within the units. Paths that only the adults can see are just unused space.

It's common to arrange classroom furniture so that it is parallel or at right angles to the nearest wall, but some diagonal furniture placement defines paths that draw people along their length and at the same time creates units that are interesting, and not necessarily rectangular. Such diagonal placement also makes the sides of the furniture available for display.

Spatial organization supports children's access to displayed literacy and materials in other ways, too. Some provisions, such as references or recording tools and materials, need to be visible from eye level for seated children in order to stimulate use of literacy in the learning activities when children are already involved; other materials such as functional print related to routines may be visible enough if they can be seen from standing eye level when children first come into the classroom.

Many teachers prefer to use the lowest space-dividing furniture in central areas and reserve the higher furniture for units nearer the walls. Children can look across the tops of low cabinets and dividers, but visual access to materials across the room is blocked by tall furniture. However, some teachers find that taller furniture can be carefully arranged in the middle of the room without blocking views of paths or essential print. High furniture also serves as a good location for common print information used by everybody throughout the day. Such arrangements are effective in settings where the seating furniture is distributed throughout the environment, rather than grouped together in one area.

Spatial Organization and Provisioning

A teacher's design for spatial organization produces the activity units and potential units for children's activity, establishing some of the work spaces that are part of the environment's provisioning pattern. Sometimes the work spaces are created quite by accident when, for instance, an opened cabinet door forms an inviting corner with a bookshelf. Children can perceive an unnoticed small, sheltered space, created where two pieces of storage furniture don't quite meet, as a work space, whether or not the teacher arranged it. Sometimes when furniture is rearranged a potential unit that has been in the environment all along is revealed as an inviting work space. For instance, turning a teacher's desk against the wall right beside a traveled path makes the knee space beneath the desk visually available as a possible work space, or a narrow space behind the classroom door, big enough for one person, may become visible to many people when a new path is located beside it. Children often like these small, unexpected work spaces when they need some time to read or write undisturbed. Provisioning with a few basic tools and materials and perhaps something comfortable to sit upon can confirm undesigned work spaces children have already found inviting.

Observations of literacy environments show a close relationship between the number of spatial divisions and the amount of current literacy materials displayed, probably because placing furniture so that it defines spatial boundaries also puts it into a position to offer display facilities on the parts of the furniture that aren't needed for materials arrangement. There seems hardly a piece of classroom furniture that can't be pressed into service for display space when it is arranged to expose the useful surfaces. The backs and sides of pianos, book racks, chests of drawers, the edges of shelving, benches, dividers, the doors of cabinets and closets, the ledges of moveable chalkboards, and the front and sides of individual desks offer essential space that supplements the more conventionally installed bulletin boards or cork strips of the architectural environment.

It seems worth examining a potential room arrangement plan for the display facilities it can offer. When the physical boundaries of activity units can also display information and provisions for that activity, arrangements are doubly effective. Teacher-displayed literacy can be distributed through the environment, rather than clustered on one or two bulletin boards, and children can make displays in the same areas where they work. Many literacy products can be well arranged in small display spaces, and displays directed to specific people are effective at lower levels. This leaves larger and more centrally visible display spaces for group-directed functional print such as daily plans. The many small display spaces created by spatial organization determine the quantity of current child-generated print that can be displayed, which both influences and is influenced by the total level of stimulus for literacy that exists in the environment.

Materials Arrangement and Spatial Organization

Decentralized material distribution is extremely important for children's involvement in literacy, and it depends upon the decentralization of the furniture that displays provisions for children's access. Teachers plan spatial organization of literacy environments with this relationship in mind. Arrangements placing all the seating furniture in one space and all the material storage furniture in another don't support a high level of stimulus for literacy activity, because children are separated from the materials and receive none of the suggestions and reminders for literacy that the provisions can offer. On the other hand, in classrooms where storage furniture and seating furniture are spread throughout the room, so all work spaces are served by nearby materials storage and display space, children are more likely to respond to the literacy stimulus presented by the materials.

Decentralizing materials storage and establishing spaces for activity occur together, because the same furniture that displays material also defines space. Decentralization produces more use of the displayed materials, and more purposeful movement within and between activity units, because children use different spaces in different ways, influ-

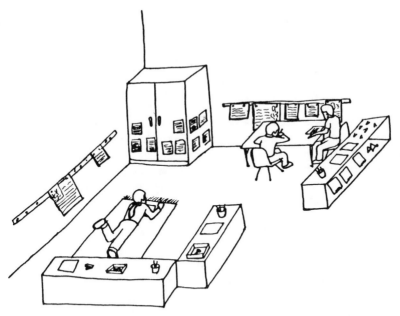

Work spaces near materials and display support literacy.

enced by the materials and their suggestions. Single central paths aren't entirely adequate for the traffic patterns that emerge, so careful organization of spaces for movement maintains shelter for working children while providing adequate access to spaces and materials without creating bottlenecks at major transition periods.

When activity units are established, one or two basic paths may be defined naturally by the storage furniture that forms some of the individual space boundaries. However, storage furniture sometimes defines shared boundaries of neighboring activity units, and paths must be provided in other ways, through the placement of dividers and standing display boards and through the locations of the openings into the units.

Bottlenecks occur when many people must approach the same piece of furniture in a very short period of time, either because there is only one place in which a person can get to some needed material or because access to all the materials storage or display space is from the same side. This is less likely to happen if storage furniture (i.e., bookcases and book racks, shelf units, cabinets) and display furniture (i.e., chart racks, standing bulletin boards, dividers, display easels) are alternated along the boundaries. Where similar shelf units or book racks are placed side by side, turning one so they face in opposite directions helps prevent bottlenecks and provides materials and display facilities for the spaces on both sides of the furniture.

Built-ins (shelving, bulletin boards, or cabinets) may create some special bottlenecks of their own if they dominate spatial-organization designs. Typically, built-ins are constructed along a single wall of a classroom, and if materials storage furniture is scarce, it might seem important to use them as the major materials arrangement center or the major location for displayed print. But to do this, the built-in side of the room would have to be arranged as a single space, centralizing both materials distribution and print display, with all its disadvantages.

Ideally, some of the built-ins would be dismantled, or spatial organization would be designed as though the built-ins did not exist, but most teachers need the potential for storage and display. However, there are alternatives to creating a single large activity unit presenting all the materials and all the print. As spaces for activity are designed, the built-ins can be incorporated into several different units by placing space-defining furniture at right angles to the built-ins and arranging partial boundaries at the front of each unit. Variations in the entrances into the units, some from the front, others from the side, clarify their distinctive appearances, so they are clearly perceived as different spaces. These arrangements have the effect of decentralizing built-in storage a little by presenting it within different activity units. Paths that are arranged to pass by the openings to the units and are alongside (rather than in front of) built-in bulletin boards help children gain access to provisions and displayed literacy materials while at the same time supporting movement through the environment and sheltering people working in these areas.

Adjoining shelf units are faced in opposite directions.

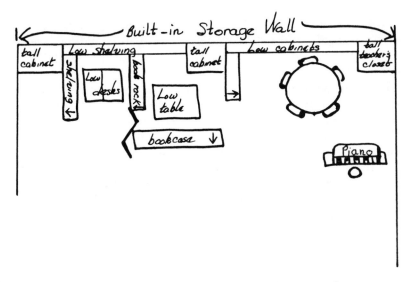

Built-ins are incorporated into different units.

Influences on Behavior

Spatial organization influences children's movement and physical behavior through strong spatial messages that urge them to move, to enter or leave areas, to pause and look at displayed print, or pass by. The messages invite children to talk, touch others or leave them alone, to hurry, or to move calmly and purposefully.

Straight-line paths from one end of a classroom to another invite hurrying, even running, so print information displayed along such paths is often unnoticed. In straight paths children may become involved in unintended socialization and lose their focus, especially if the path's edges aren't well defined and entrances into the bordering activity units are vague. Paths that change direction invite slower and more focused movement. Diagonally turning paths seem to make children aware of more spaces and materials than do those that turn at right angles, and displays of information along the turning paths are usually noticed and used. The turning paths also seem to draw people along from one place to another, rather than encouraging them to socialize and lose the focus of their activity.

The amount of intrusion children experience in their work spaces and activity units is closely related to children's attention span and to the appearance of restlessness. Where surrounding spaces of units overlap or paths direct moving people into surrounding spaces of activity units, children in the units appear easily distractible because of the intrusion.

Spatial organization also influences the amount of interest shown toward provisions for literacy activity, and whether or not they are used at all, to such an extent that teachers can be convinced that children have no interest in literacy activity or displayed print. This happens often when the arrangement of storage and display furniture places the materials completely out of children's view, even though the teacher may be able to see them quite plainly, or when there are no clear paths that lead to the materials and provide physical access to them. A different set of arrangements can elicit behaviors indicating that those same children would rather engage in literacy than any other form of activity and that their work revolves around books and print.

SPACE AND LITERACY CHARACTERISTICS

Spatial organization has an indirect, but essential, role to play in establishing several of the characteristics of the literacy environment discussed in an earlier chapter. The presence of *interesting things to read and write about, recording tools and materials, books everywhere,* and *references where they are needed* all require spatial organization that makes materials storage available throughout the environment and enhances visibility of the displayed materials and posted print. The decentralized arrangement of storage furniture supports the distribution of these important literacy provisions, and clear paths defined by that furniture arrangement support children's awareness and interest in those materials.

Spatial organization establishes other literacy characteristics more directly, because it is through the placement of furniture and the definition of spaces that they are made available. Creating spaces for reading and writing is the basic task of spatial organization, and the space dividers that accomplish that task also provide many of the environment's *display spaces and display tools* when the backs and sides of the furniture are made available for display, and display tools are attached.

5

The Functional Use of Print

Functional print plays an important role in organizing classroom life. In the broadest sense, print is functional when it is associated with meaning (Jewell & Zintz, 1986). Fluent readers may sometimes scan print without perceiving any meaning, especially when the print uses an unfamiliar language or orthography, but usually print in one's own language is seen as message. As very young children begin to understand the functions of symbols and print, they may sometimes perceive and use letters as designs, unconnected with specific meaning, yet at other times assign meaning to holistic symbols and logos that include letters. For mature as well as just beginning readers, print is functional when it carries meaning for the person who sees it. Without that meaning it is only design.

There is also a more specific way of defining functional print. In today's world functional print helps a person know what to do: It offers specific information needed to function in a situation; it guides activity or behavior; and it registers personal information. Involvement with functional print is often brief, meeting an immediate need, and may take the form of writing or of reading. Writing functional print is a part of everyday activities such as making labels, preparing lists, writing checks, and noting addresses and telephone numbers. Records of meetings and expenses, designs and plans, library borrowing, inventories, and voter registration are a few of the familiar functional uses of writing that accompany daily life. Reading print as diverse as road signs, directions on coin telephones, bus schedules, or ballots is a normal part of living in a complex society. Warnings of toxic materials and washed-out roads direct behavior; advertisements and price lists influence decisions; contracts, written agreements, and rule books clarify what is to be done under certain circumstances. The functional uses of print enable people to negotiate comfortably both familiar and unfamiliar situations as they go about their daily business.

School settings can involve children extensively in functional uses of print in ways that resemble the practical and ever-present literacy environment of adults. Such an environment offers materials and information to sustain children's interests, making materials, and visible forms of literacy readily available. Time and opportunity for personal engagement with learning activities and explorations are provided, and the information necessary to function in the environment is made public through displayed print.

THE EASEL SQUABBLE

The kindergarten teachers wanted self-selection to be a cooperative and satisfying time when the children were all intensely involved with learning activities of their choice. But one day in October, another noisy argument at the painting easel again demanded a teacher's intervention. The easel area was crowded with kindergarten children quarreling about turns. Two demanded that another vacate the easel so they could have a turn, but the painter wouldn't leave because his painting wasn't finished; the waiting children rushed toward one of the teachers to complain.

It was the end of the day before the teachers had time to talk about the turn-taking problems. The easel could accommodate two children at a time, because it had two sides, but painting was an activity that everybody liked, and turns were in high demand. Painting has a good deal of holding power, so children stayed involved for a fairly long time, making it hard for others to wait their turn. The children needed some way of knowing their turn would come, so they would stop hovering over the painters.

The teachers didn't want to solve the problem by assigning turns for all the activities because helping children learn to manage their own activities was an important goal for the program. Another important goal was the development of the social skills needed for functioning in a group setting. They decided to combine those goals with a third, getting children involved in literacy as part of their daily lives, while at the same time helping resolve the easel squabble. Children needed to manage choices, take turns, and share space amicably through some use of functional print. The teachers chose to support those processes by setting up functional sign-on charts so children could record their names and see the names of other children in print. The children could also consult the chart to predict when their turns would occur.

At the easel area a long sheet of paper titled "Easel" was displayed, and a paper cup containing two markers was tacked beside it. The teachers decided to wait until a problem arose before presenting the chart to the children. Soon after the self-selection period began, two children were painting, and three were waiting impatiently. As those who waited began to press the painters to hurry, the teacher suggested there was a way to keep track of whose turn was next, so they wouldn't have to stand in the area while waiting. She showed the chart's title and explained that they could write their names under "Easel," and that the person whose name was closest to the top of the page would have the next turn. To model this, she wrote the names of the current painters at the top of the page with one of the markers, then returned it to its container, saying, "Now you can write your names." One child could do this without assistance, and the others brought name cards to the easel area for reference. By the time their names were on the chart, one of the painters had finished. The teacher asked him to draw a line through his name, showing that a place at the easel was now available for the next person on the list. When that person was settled down for work, the teacher pointed out to the waiting children that they could ask one of the painters to notify them when their turn came, and meanwhile they could work elsewhere. She reminded them that if their turn didn't occur on the very day they signed, they could be sure of a turn in the next day or two, since the same chart would be there until everybody who chose the easel had a turn.

In two days, the easel sign-on chart was working smoothly, and the children understood how to arrange for a turn. Children knew where their names were on the list, and some were reading the names that preceded theirs so they could ask to be called for their turns.

FUNCTIONAL PRINT IN THE ENVIRONMENT

A basic goal for learners in any curriculum for literacy is the association of print with meaning, and the anticipation of the presence of meaning wherever they see the written word (Smith, 1978). In this sense, all aspects of a classroom's literacy environment can contribute to the understanding of functional print. It is important for children to attach meaning to print and to become accustomed to using print to get along in society. This goal is approached in instructional programs and is extended by the functioning literacy environment.

In a more specific way, it is also important for children to find it necessary to use print in order to function through the school day and

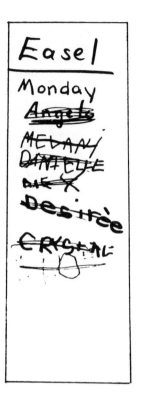

A sign-on chart helped children wait their turns.

to find ways to relate this meaningful print to personal uses in their larger environment outside the school. Children moving into literacy are very active in using symbols for their own purposes; they may practice something they have just learned or they may reorganize and extend already acquired competencies. However, they do not necessarily become involved with daily functional uses of print in their classrooms unless environments are arranged for that purpose, demanding the use of print and responding to events through print.

By design, functional literacy environments make it necessary for children to make use of some forms of reading and writing all day because most of the guidance and direction for the day's work is presented in symbols and print. When functional print is connected with events that have strong personal meaning for the children, the need to use literacy is intensified. An aggressive quest for meaning (Holdaway, 1980) is a characteristic of children's encounters with print as they seek the information needed to negotiate their day, and children and teachers together make the functional use of print a way of life in the environment.

Current, clearly displayed print helps everybody know what to do and how to do it, offers specific information needed to function in a situation, and guides activity or behavior in some way. It is necessary to attend to functional print in order to go through the school day, so this print creates a demand for reading. At the same time children make independent use of the environment and participate comfortably in the events of the day, because the information they need to do so is available at all times. Print is functional in the classroom only when its message applies to events and arrangements on the day it is read, because its function is to guide activity or behavior appropriately. Yesterday's schedule is not very helpful about what to do today.

Management procedures demanding the use of literacy to negotiate the day result from thoughtful planning by teachers. Beginning with the more obvious functions of schedule following, keeping track of one's own job responsibilities, and being able to find materials in the environment, the uses of literacy expand as announcements are gradually replaced by symbols and print, so children learn to search out needed information, knowing they will find it somewhere in the environment. Over time, more and more information becomes public in print form and stays on display as long as it is current, so children develop the habit of referring to it. Most of the information needed for knowing what will happen, where learning materials belong, how they are used, what one is supposed to do, and with whom is available to everyone. As days function more smoothly, children become better able to manage their time, to look ahead and prepare for scheduled events, or to take care of many simple questions and provisioning needs by locating relevant information and acting upon it. What begins as a deliberate environmental arrangement to demand children's use of literacy soon produces positive side effects in self-management and independence.

Teachers produce most of the functional print in the environment when it is first established, but children soon begin to contribute. Their role in the production of functional print varies in different settings, and there are several ways they can participate. Sometimes children prepare and display the day's schedules or messages about routines; often they take care of daily updating of information about regular events by changing or adjusting the print as appropriate; and sometimes they prepare functional labels for provisions or displays in the environment.

Announcements are replaced by symbols and print.

It is useful for the person who writes functional print to date it and also sign it, so any reader can check to see if it is current, or go to the writer for clarification. Signing announcements, schedules, or lists of procedures is also a courtesy that tends to carry over into other kinds of displayed print.

Daily Routines

The overall plan for the day provides a good focus for functional print, especially when the information is available in some consistent location when children arrive at the beginning of the day. Schedules, lists of group members and their activities, and special plans and assignments attract attention because the information applies to everyone in the environment. Important information is often presented pictorially as well as in print to accommodate the different literacy levels in any group and help give meaning to the print. There are many places for this information. It can be displayed on surfaces like the lower part of a bulletin board, a chart stand in the center of the room, a wall beneath a chalkboard near a large group area, or a divider. Materials posted right at the door are noticeable immediately when children come in, but tend to be out of view the rest of the day. Plans are easier to consult if they are visible from many locations, or if they are in a place where they can be seen by many people at once as children move into the environment.

Information about routines displayed around the environment can be used by individuals as they work. Calendars and prearranged turn schedules are changed in the work areas in preparation for each day, and inventory lists are available to check and replenish the environment at the end of the day.

Regular morning routines often are managed through functional print, as children check in, record whether they will eat the school lunch, purchase lunch tickets, and return permission slips. They sign in appropriate places, or move labeled markers from one location to another, or place envelopes and slips into particular containers as directed by written information. Children enter weather observations onto a record sheet; sometimes they tally the names on sign-in sheets and make out forms to report attendance to the school office. In countless classrooms they read and take action, record, sign, count, and report as they use functional print to begin their day.

Labeling

A label is a special kind of functional print used to identify or explain nearby materials. Teachers in literacy environments label learning materials and equipment that are visible in open holders,

Functional print directs morning routines.

rather than in closed boxes that conceal contents. The nonprint materials give meaning to the print so the information becomes available to beginning readers as well as those who are more fluent. The materials arrangement and the associated print provide all the information needed to locate provisions or to put them away.

A label reading "pencils" doesn't mean much when it is attached to a box holding pieces of styrofoam; however, materials do get misplaced and sometimes empty containers are pressed hurriedly into service despite the mismatched labels. With label blanks and recording tools visible and close at hand, children or teachers can notice and make necessary changes so labels become functional again.

Labels are often written in sentence form (These magazines have Christmas pictures you can cut out), rather than as a single word. This is especially helpful because the sentence form gives more information about the materials and their possible uses, and it is also helpful because the sentences on the labels call forth reading behaviors much like those used in other reading situations.

Sentence labels
are helpful.

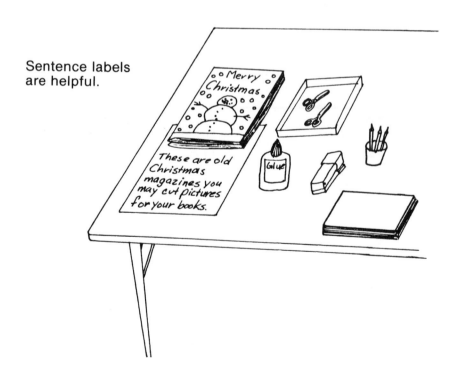

Child-written labels are often connected with the display of their own work, or with materials they wish to share or call to the attention of classmates. At the simplest level, children label personal materials with their own names, but as they grow in uses of literacy, children label their own displays with additional information and also prepare labels to clarify placement and use of classroom provisions.

Sometimes brief directions for making an object displayed by one child encourages extended interest from others. In some instances, children prepare a special form of sign-on chart, asking for a written response to their display. Placing a written tool beside the chart strengthens the request.

Functional Sign-on Charts

The response request described above is an example of the sign-on charts that appear in many different forms in literacy environments. Prepared by teachers or children, such charts provide a format with a written question or statement and a request for written responses, with space for these responses.

Functional sign-on charts are used for routines and management, and they serve many purposes: checking materials in and out, announcing schedule changes with requests to "sign here after you've read this," putting out calls for misplaced objects, verifying completed tasks, recording turns, registering choices, calling for job volunteers. The first few responses on the chart draw attention to the information, and participation attracts other children to the displayed chart to add their responses.

Children also prepare sign-on charts to gather suggestions about matters of concern to the group. These quickly prepared forms of functional print are powerful because they call for an immediate response and because they engage children in writing as well as reading. At the same time, sign-ons encourage children to share information that can help everybody function throughout the day.

Displayed Directions

Task cards and other directions for activities or procedures function as invitations as well as information, calling attention to their contents and engaging children's interest. They also add a social dimension to the functional use of print because all the steps of an activity are made public through displayed directions, and friendly

Sign-on charts call for writing as well as reading.

onlookers can offer assistance (whether or not it is needed or wanted!). Information about interesting activities becomes widely shared.

Displayed directions provide a variety of procedural information. Clearly stated how-to information about using equipment, focusing a projector, rewinding an extension cord, or protecting a work surface is displayed where it will be used. Directions for checking library books, obtaining the hall pass, making lunch count, exiting safely in fire drills, or replacing provisions enable children to help one another perform routine tasks without teacher assistance. Procedures for some teacher-designed activities are also displayed, making it possible to gather materials and engage in and complete an activity without the teacher's step-by-step supervision.

Recipes, in the form of displayed directions, are especially interesting to children. Complex recipes, such as those for cooking, call for planning and scheduling so that necessary ingredients and equipment can be gathered. Even if the recipe is used only once, it is often left on display throughout the planning (even over a period of several days, if needed), gathering, cooking, and sharing stages of the activity. Other recipes, such as the formula for mixing easel paint, plant food solutions, or a proper meal for a gerbil, remain on display as long as those in the environment have responsibilities that require the use of that information.

Record Keeping

Ordinarily record keeping is seen as a teacher's responsibility, but making written records to keep track of information useful to the group establishes another functional use of print for children. Observing and recording playground conditions, times of day when the sun causes a glare in different areas of the environment, or other events affecting the group's activities offer insight for group planning. Record keeping can occur independently when recording materials and clearly displayed directions are located where an event is to be observed. List paper, a record book, a computer, a chalkboard, or a tape recorder are all useful when children begin to record and compile information. These provide alternate ways of entering and reviewing records.

Because it is necessary for record keeping to be functional, the records are reviewed periodically and their information is used in some practical way. Records of days and times that plants are watered and records of the amount of plant food used each time plants are fertilized may explain what is happening to their blooms. On the basis of those records, watering and feeding schedules for plants can be organized or changed. Other classroom records are practical for children's problem solving and group decision making. For instance, check-out records of playground equipment are helpful when some children claim they never get a turn. With the records, children can see which people use the equipment regularly and which don't. If the same few children always get to the playground balls first, the record will support the argument for more sharing, and decisions about new arrangements can be made. Records of the quantity of construction paper used to replace provisions each day, or the amount of food consumed by a classroom animal, produce data children can use for planning as they make provisioning lists or inventories.

Functional review of records involves children in reading the records as well as writing them. There is great variety in the contents of records and in the information-gathering procedures for a classroom group, and all serve to help children identify and take some responsibility for meeting problems or needs in the physical and social setting of the environment.

Combining Print with Other Forms of Information

Extensive use of functional print makes information public and stimulates children's use of literacy. Naturally, there are children in every group who don't independently read everything they encounter, so peer help is especially useful in calling attention to the print, interpreting its information, and modeling the uses of print. At the same time, children can be moved toward independence in interpreting functional print through combinations of print with pictures or other symbolic information.

Displayed directions often combine print with pictures, or samples of materials to be used, or sketches of the necessary actions (much like the drawings in appliance manuals) in an effort to clarify print. Similar arrangements of pictures or objects with nearby related print are designed to emphasize the value of the information offered in print.

ENCOURAGING CHILDREN'S INVOLVEMENT

Much of the teacher's work of initiating and maintaining the active use of functional print in the environment is done behind the scenes, but some of it is carried out during the day when both children and

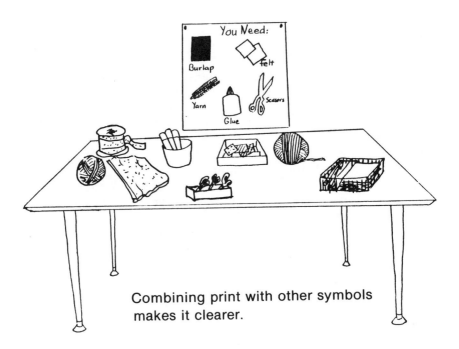

Combining print with other symbols
makes it clearer.

teachers use the environment. Teachers encourage the use of displayed functional print through modeling or interactions with children and by writing and displaying functional information during the day, at the time and place to be used by children.

Interactions

Many teachers encourage children toward the functional use of print by referring them to displayed information in response to questions about schedules or routines. It may be important to show a particular child where the information is displayed and perhaps give some assistance in reading it. At other times a reminder that the information is available is enough. Although it might be faster to answer children's questions than to help them locate and read the information, teachers who work in this way to establish a demand for literacy find that the time spent leading individuals to functional print decreases as children begin to realize its value.

Throughout the day, certain teacher actions can encourage a small group of children to develop functional information. This might be a proposal for a schedule change, or a plan of action for some project they want to initiate, or arrangements for record-keeping procedures. Once the information is fairly well developed, the teacher's next discussion with those children encourages them to put it into print, making it public so others have access to it.

Helping a person check a classroom record, suggesting that someone review a set of directions to see whether necessary procedures have been carried out, taking a moment to acknowledge an individual who has been able to organize a morning's work by referring to functional print, and calling attention to new functional print are the types of brief interactions in which the teacher responds to children within the context of their own activity. Teachers keep uses of functional print alive as they help, suggest, encourage, question, point out, and acknowledge children's practical uses of print.

In response to child-identified problems with day-to-day life in the environment, such as a scarcity of material, access problems for high-demand equipment, or interference with work, teachers take advantage of the literacy potential in problem solving. They encourage children to put the pertinent information into print so all can act upon it to relieve the problem situation. Teachers also remain alert to opportunities for incorporating literacy into other activities and contexts that have importance and practical meaning to the children.

Modeling

To help them perceive the utility of literacy, children need people around them who model extensive use of print in functional ways. At first, their teacher is the model most available during the school day. Over time children become increasingly involved in the use of print and become models for one another; however, teachers remain important models. Even though they continue to add print to the environment when the children are not present, children need to observe teachers in the process of writing and displaying information during the day. When teachers model use of displayed functional print for information while the children are present, they convey through their behavior the utility of print information and the importance of seeking it out.

Teachers therefore seek opportunities to be seen using functional print and are deliberate in being sure their literacy activity is visible. This modeling is done in a natural way that makes sense in the context, but it is done quite consciously. For instance, a teacher may walk up to displayed print, read it, or run a finger down a schedule, or in some other way make the consulting of the print obvious.

Time for Functional Use of Print

In a functioning literacy environment the day is organized to replace blocks of time reserved for verbal announcements and directions with access to announcements and directions in print. Children's use of functional print doesn't require extra time, but it does call for different uses of time throughout the day.

The times of day when children enter the environment from recess, lunch, and special classes are important opportunities for the use of literacy, because they need to consult functional print in order to refocus on their work, find out what to do next, or see how much time is available for an activity. There are other transition periods that occur as everybody moves from one setting to another within the environment, such as shifting from a group meeting to independent work, from a work session to lunchtime, from self-selection to story time. These are equally valuable opportunities to use literacy, and children consult and produce print in the process of cleaning up, bringing activity to a close, displaying products, or reviewing schedules and responsibilities.

Seen in this light, a transition period is as useful for literacy growth as any other period of the day, if sufficient time is provided. Time that might otherwise be spent in getting all members of the class to attend to instructions and in making verbal announcements is available for individuals to gather information, change focus, settle down to work, or finish a project. And there is also time to sign, display, report, or check off completed work. Through functional print and the time to use it, children accomplish these tasks on their own, or with the help of their peers. In addition to the time provided for the transition itself, reminders that the transition is coming are offered in some way: An abbreviated form of the day's schedule is displayed beside a highly visible classroom clock, a message is written on a chalkboard a few minutes before the end of a period, or a teacher begins to model appropriate finishing-up behaviors. Children are alerted to the coming shift of activities, and the different paces of individuals are accommodated, as children wind up their work or prepare it for continuation at another time.

When print is the source of information about the day, it is possible for anybody who enters the environment to move into the day's activities right away. In many literacy environments, individual children function during the beginning of the day much as they do during any transition, and large group meetings, occurring later in the morning, are used for a different type of sharing and discussing than might otherwise be possible.

ENVIRONMENTAL EVIDENCE OF CHILDREN'S PROGRESS

Keeping track of children's progress in literacy is a complex task that draws upon information from many sources. The interpretation of each set of data is informed by the teacher's knowledge of individuals, based on information from other sources. Of course, teachers have much more than environmental data to help them keep track of children's literacy, but the environment provides information offering some special insights into children's growth in the functional uses of print.

At the end of the day, children leave behind them a wealth of information about their understanding of functional print and their ability to make use of it; that information is present in concrete and visible form in the products and messages of the environment. In addition to the materials that present useful information, from time to time throughout the day a teacher catches glimpses of children engaged in functional uses of print as they make use of the environment's resources for their work. The observations of children negotiating the day with the help of print are quite brief and may be planned or unplanned. But when teachers direct their attention to children functioning in the environment, these focused glimpses provide very clear views of children's ability to make use of print for practical purposes.

Reading the Environment

Walking through the environment regularly, reading the functional print children have produced, and looking for evidence of their ability to act upon it put the teacher in touch with important information for building a picture of children's understanding of print and their competence in using it.

One of the questions that focuses the teacher's daily reading of the environment is which children are producing functional print for the group and which are not yet doing this. The signatures on the dated functional print on display provide this information. A simple record sheet consisting of a class list on lined paper makes it easy to put a date or a check mark beside the appropriate name for each new piece of functional print, and periodic review of the record helps the teacher see which individuals are contributing.

How well the entire group of children understands and acts on the functional print that directs daily routines is another focusing question. This can easily be seen as the teacher reviews sign-on charts about routines to see what necessary information has been entered for the day; looks through materials storage areas to see if labels and materials still match; and checks provisioning in different areas to see which supplies have been replenished as called for by provisioning inventories. The environment is inspected for evidence that posted jobs have been suitably completed, materials put where they belong, and cleanup tasks finished. With this reading of the environment the teacher gains insight into the group's progress with the mutually understood uses of functional print.

Work on display in the environment or preserved for completion on another day offers information about a specific child's ability to make use of procedural print. Work can be compared with displayed directions or procedures to determine understanding of the process presented in print. Reviewing children's materials also shows which individuals select and independently carry out activities from displayed directions, and which do not seem to be attracted to such experiences.

Observing Children

During the day, as children work in the literacy environment, a teacher sees and notes individuals in action and hears children as they help one another. Particularly helpful information about children's ability to make use of functional print comes from observations of peer assistance, children using print, and children's actions in response to print information.

Watching children help one another interpret functional print is quite revealing. Teachers notice who does the asking, who does the helping, and the particular situations in which help is most often needed in a given day. Although there may not be time to record what is seen, information consciously noted can be reviewed later. When there is time to reflect on peer interactions, the particular questions asked and the answers given can provide considerable insight into children's growth.

As children work their way through the routines of the day, observations of the uses of functional print reveal which children are actually reading the print and which children are getting their information by watching the actions of others. Some children are drawn to information as soon as it is posted; they are eager to know what they will be doing, with whom, and for how long. Others may be using functional print only to find their names and the names of friends and seek the rest of the information in other ways. There may be children who produce print about routines and procedures during the day in an attempt to help people or even to persuade the rest of the group to do things their way.

Children's actions within the literacy environment also offer useful information about their competence in the functional use of print. For many, knowing what to do and when, as informed by the displayed print, is an accomplishment. Others go further in their uses of print, demonstrating that specific information is read and used as they go to posted meeting places at appointed times for special events, arrive at instructional group sessions with all the print-announced materials, or comment upon changed plans and schedules.

Shared Personal Communication

In our society literacy continues to be very important, even as new developments in telecommunications increase the availability of alternative methods of personal communication. Literacy is used for private personal communication to individuals, in notes, memos, and letters; it is used for public personal communication as well, in on-line computer networks, in letters to the editor, and in other publicly shared statements. The social context of personal communication resembles that of oral language, because it is usually directed from one individual to another, or from one person to a small group of people known to one another or with common interests (Jewell & Zintz, 1986).

In personal communication, the message is from one individual to another individual, or to a group. The intended audience is known to the sender, either personally or through shared interests and experiences, and the sender is known to the recipients in the same way. The message is personal in that it deals with matters that concern the sender, or that are believed to be of personal concern to the recipient. Usually, but not always, written personal communication is addressed to someone who is not present at the time of the writing.

The classroom, with its long-term association of a group of people who share daily experiences and come to know one another well, provides a natural setting for personal communication. Usually, people who spend most of their time near one another use oral language for personal communication; however, written messages also play a role in those settings. Even in the intimacy of the family some parents use written communication to their children, for instance, when they can't speak to them directly because the children are out of the house or settled down for the night, or when complex schedules keep family members coming and going at different times, establishing a need for reminders of appointments and responsibilities. Children frequently use written personal communication to tell their parents of their feelings and plans; they write letters of explanations and intentions, or create special-event messages, such as birthday cards or valentines (Taylor, 1973).

Children who have used such written personal communication at home find a setting within the learning environment where they are encouraged to extend their uses of literacy for message writing. At the same time, arrangements in the classroom provide suggestions and models for children whose home experiences haven't involved them in written communication. The environment is arranged to help children become accustomed to the use of writing as a dimension of social interaction and to connect literacy with matters and events that have intense personal meaning.

Communications shared by placing them in a public place are no less personal because they aren't private, particularly when those who are likely to see and read the message are friends of the sender and recipient. They are personal because they are written by an individual for an individual or set of people to whom the message is important. Environmental suggestions for shared personal communication encourage children to produce private messages. However, shared communications play a special role in the literacy environment because, when posted, they too become part of the surrounding stimulus for the use of literacy. Children who see other people's messages are reminded that they can use print in this way; so they send messages to the teacher and to one another, look for personal messages around the room, and read, answer, and act upon messages sent to them.

Personal communication has immediate relevance, because each message has a brief but potent life and is replaced with another soon after it is received. This dynamic aspect of shared personal communication seems to bring the literacy environment to life, reflecting the spirit of the children who work in it and the flow of social relationships and events that are part of their lives as active learners.

PLEASE DON'T INTERRUPT!

On Tuesday, Mrs. Plants lost her patience completely, as one child after another came to the area where she was working with a small group, to tell her something that could have waited, ask a question they could answer themselves, or complain about what somebody else was doing. Each interruption affected the group's attention and distracted her, too, even if she stopped only long enough to ask children not to interrupt again. Finally, in desperation, she responded to one person loudly enough to be heard by most of the children: "I can't stop to talk to you when I'm with a group. If it's important, write me a note and I'll get back to you! PLEASE DON'T INTERRUPT ME AGAIN!"

The remaining ten minutes of work with the group was peaceful, with no interruptions, although Mrs. Plants saw out of the corner of her eye several tiptoe trips to the bulletin board near the group area and was aware that some children were tacking small pieces of paper onto it. When she had a moment to look, after the group work was over, she found four written messages. One said, "I need help," another said, "My mother is coming for me after the lunch recess," and the other two asked to use the playground ball during afternoon recess. None of the notes was signed, but the teacher knew the children well enough to identify the writers.

As she looked at the notes, the teacher was a little embarrassed. She had impulsively blurted out the writing suggestion without serious thought, and there was a bit of sarcasm in the phrase "I'll get back to you." However, her impulse had turned out well, and the suggestions had already involved some children who had not previously shown much interest in writing. She saw that the person who requested help had solved the problem alone or found help from another student, so she decided not to respond immediately to the unsigned notes. The class meeting just before lunch would be a good time to discuss message writing as an alternative to interrupting the teacher.

When the class was together, Mrs. Plants mentioned the four notes people had left her and expressed appreciation for their courtesy in not interrupting her or the group. "But I wasn't able to answer the notes," she commented, "because they weren't signed, so they didn't tell me who to respond to." The discussion about writing notes and signing them so the teacher could answer the appropriate person continued for a short time, and the group moved on to other business.

On Wednesday, at the end of the small-group period, there were even more messages on the bulletin board, and the groups hadn't been interrupted at all. Each note was signed, and the teacher spoke to several people whose question or request was urgent and wrote a response across the bottom of two notes that weren't so pressing.

By Friday the bulletin board was almost covered with notes, which had accumulated day by day. Mrs. Plants spoke to three or four children, as if in response to their notes that were still on display, although they had been written two days before. They were puzzled until she showed them their old, undated notes; later they were ready to propose a solution to that confusion during the group's business meeting. They suggested that everybody put the date on their notes, just like on a letter, and also take down the note as soon as they received an answer. They also proposed that anybody who wanted the space could remove notes that were at least one day old.

For several days, every message posted on the bulletin board near the group area was directed to Mrs. Plants. Then, about the middle of the following week, messages apparently directed to children working in the small groups began to appear, such as "Will you let me use your silver marker?" or "Do you want to play with me at recess?" The messages had been tacked beside the group area by the writers, who also made elaborate silent signals to the individuals addressed. The teacher treated the messages as though directed at her, explaining to one child that she didn't have a silver marker and to another that she would be busy during recess; so once again the written messages came up for discussion in the class meeting, and the need to address personal communications was clearly seen by everyone.

As children's written personal communications continued, Mrs. Plants began to write personal messages herself: "Vittorio, does the new baby wake you up in the middle of the night when she gets hungry?" or "Maggie, did you finish the story about the dinosaur yet? I'd like to know how it all ends." Similar personal notes were waiting in some display area near their tables when everybody arrived in the morning. The teacher also began to write responses to many of the children's questions during the day, although some called for a more direct exchange with the writers.

The children's interest in message writing continued to grow, so Mrs. Plants added a central message board to the environment. She placed half-sheet memo forms from the school office in one area of the classroom, with headings for date, sender, and addressee on each one. Small, opened boxes holding memo-sized paper were available in every other area, with small assortments of working pens, sharpened pencils, and fine-line markers. Children posted and removed dated and addressed personal messages from the message board with regularity, and more communications began to appear in other locations. Messages for individuals appeared taped to the edge of an addressee's desk, or fastened to furniture in the same area.

The teacher often thought of her exasperated response to children's interruptions that had triggered the widespread use of personal communication in the classroom. Although it hadn't been a consciously planned response, it certainly had been effective and would become deliberate strategy in the future, since it had promoted so much literacy activity.

CHILDREN'S COMMUNICATIONS

Children's daily use of print messages enlivens the literacy environment, because each message is interesting and important for the children involved in the communication, and their messages make important contributions to the quantity and variety of the environment's print. Almost any event in the school day provides something to write about. Children make appointments and requests, comment upon one another's work and activities, report their own activities, make personal announcements, express affection for someone, or build social bonds through written communications.

Appointments

There are always reasons for children to make appointments in classrooms when time is provided for people to act upon the environment's suggestions for activity. Appointment communications are usually directed from one individual to another, or one person may try to get a group together at a certain time, in which case the message addresses more than two people.

Some appointment notes are related to functional print, because they are about classroom business. For instance, a child makes an appointment with another to clean out the block area after lunch, or someone asks another child to help make a new sign for the Current Events bulletin board during the work period in the morning. Through such "business" appointments, children sharing responsibilities for maintaining the environment look ahead in their day and plan when to carry them out. Other appointment notes are directed to the teacher: conference appointments, appointments to pick up special supplies needing a teacher's check-out signature, reminders to the teacher that a child will be leaving to keep an appointment with the librarian.

Some appointment notes are social rather than business related. A child may write a reminder to someone about a promised sharing of a jump rope during recess, or make an appointment to walk to a scout meeting after school, or to eat lunch together.

The use of written appointments is supported by information sources such as calendars, posted schedules, and clocks and by some interesting recording materials such as appointment books, appointment forms, and a variety of small notepaper. Sign-ons with time slots that encourage children to set their appointments for work with the teacher are useful, especially when they also request a note to the teacher as a reminder.

Dear Students ages from 6-13,

If you would like to join in summer league baseball program meet me after School on Monday. Your teacher will give a sighn up sheet before you go home today. Bring it back Monday if you can play.

Robby Martin

Children write personal appointment messages.

Requests

Calls for materials appear frequently on message boards. These request communications are often directed to the group, so addressees aren't named, but they come from specifically identified individuals, so responses can be made to the writer. Children call for raw materials that are not part of school supplies (corrugated cardboard, carpentry wood, Styrofoam) or for special equipment such as a compass or a T-square. Requests for information also appear, sometimes directed to specific people seen by the writer as likely to have information to share, sometimes addressed to the group. Children may ask where to find a document, tool, or material; they may ask for information or references about a topic they are studying; or they may request information about dates and places for community events.

Sometimes children's messages ask for general assistance with their day's work, and sometimes help requests are quite specific. Children also ask permission: they write messages to a friend for permission to borrow, to the teacher to check on an appropriate time to go out after information or materials, or to a specific group for permission to change a group-planned product.

The same arrangements that stimulate other kinds of personal communications are effective for written requests. Recording tools and materials and many display spaces, all well distributed, are important. The presence of interesting things in the environment to read and write about and models of written requests and provisions are important, too. Children's perception of a day's work centers on the information, objects, and products with which they are involved, and it is often these focusing materials that generate needs leading to request communications.

Commentary

Comments about events, activities, and projects are a normal part of life when a group of people spend their days working together. The comments take the form of appreciations and complaints, and expressions of approval or disapproval of something that has occurred. When the people concerned are children, some channeling of commentary is often needed, to support positive experiences and relationships and protect vulnerable self-concepts. Legitimizing productive commentary through the literacy environment is a helpful way to do this, provided the social climate within the group has been carefully developed through a variety of shared, teacher-mediated experiences and is basically supportive to individuals.

Notes of appreciation for displayed projects or creative work usually appear first, especially when there is some modeling of such communications by the teacher. These messages are written by indi-

I nead halp plees

Lynette

Some communications are requests.

viduals and directed to a specific person, and they are received with delight. In some classrooms, where peer relationships and social skills are well developed, students may write letters of complaint, directing them to specific individuals, asking them to change their ways. One person complains to another about feet in the path causing the writer to stumble, or somebody writes a note addressed to a pair who always overstay the agreed-upon time at the computer, so that others don't have a turn. Responses to complaint messages take several forms, including messages of agreement, defense, denial, or appeals to the teacher for intervention. The social behaviors aren't very different from those involved with verbal complaints and responses, but using written communication offers the added dimension of taking some time to think before complaining or responding, and it maintains children's engagement in literacy.

Commentary isn't always about people, however. Children often use these messages to make jokes about some shared event, to comment to a friend about a television program or book both have experienced, or to comment upon the day in general and special events that occur.

In addition to the materials that encourage most forms of literacy, models of commentary messages are important, especially as they influence the way children deliver critical commentary. The frequent presence of approval and appreciation messages written to individuals places the emphasis on positive commentary, and where critical comments are acceptable, models that are clear and informative, or touched with humor, help children be responsible in their personal communications.

Social Contact

Elementary children are very involved in social relationships: building social bonds, wanting a best friend, expressing affection and sympathy, building a peer group (Rubin, 1980). They often make use of literacy in hidden ways in the classroom, with secret messages, codes, and private lists; these undercover literacy activities usually involve making and establishing social contact with peers. Children exchange notes, they make and gather lists of names for clubs or gangs, and they collect votes on various matters such as color preferences and favorite foods. Private social communications are natural for children at these developmental levels, but the exclusion of some and the inclusion of others that are often part of building peer groups can be painful for individuals and disruptive to a supportive, cooperative classroom setting. However, shared social communications, encouraged and redi-

The Indian home is made out of adobe. My home is not. Are Fire Place is not There to help us see It is There for The winter.

You answered well how your homes were different. I notice you didn't say how they were alike - or did you not think that they are alike in any way?

Nice!

Commentary messages help children in their work.

rected toward common interests and experiences related to the class-room group, provide a useful outlet for that reaching out for peer contact and expand the uses of literacy within social relationships. Children collect phone numbers and addresses of all class members, ask others to sign petitions, start a new club organized around a special interest (such as a carpentry club) through written personal communications.

Children take great pleasure in writing shared messages of affection and sympathy to others; they write birthday cards, good-bye cards, valentines, sick cards, and "like" letters to one another and the teacher. Clever wording, special illustrations, or new ways of folding the paper containing the message are noticed when these personal communications are shared, and often become common practice within the group.

A box of recycled memo paper and a handful of writing tools by the exit door make it possible for children to use literacy for personal communications during a recess period, and well-distributed arrangements of provisions for illustrating, writing, and display support shared social communications. Models of messages and sign-ons for gathering social information set the framework for this form of communication and help children draw upon their social interests in ways that support the total group climate, while using literacy for their own purposes.

Personal Announcements

Children often come to school excited about something that has happened in their homes or community; these events are personally important, and they want to share them, so they write personal announcements directed to the group. The personal announcements are usually about the writers themselves or about people and events close to them, such as special visitors at home, a new baby, an award or achievement, a family move, an impending trip, and some are even written about personal experiences in school. Sometimes personal announcements are written by one person, but are about another individual known to the group.

In addition to other provisions and arrangements for literacy, some announcements are stimulated by stationery, in the form of no-message cards, small folded notepaper, and printed announcement cards that offer a variety of models and possibilities.

Reporting

Report messages about how something was done, what information was obtained, or how many tasks were accomplished grow out of cooperative relationships and shared work or interests. They are written because an individual has a commitment to accomplish something for some purpose important to a group, and that commitment is personally felt rather than an imposed obligation. The environmental arrangements that lead to writing personal communications for reporting go beyond suggestions for particular forms of communication. Information sources offer content for cooperative study and for literacy activity, spatial organization encourages group efforts, and display arrangements within group work spaces provide space for work-in-progress. All of these arrangements support spontaneous involvement in focused group activity, which in turn stimulates the commitment that makes shared personal communication a vehicle for reporting.

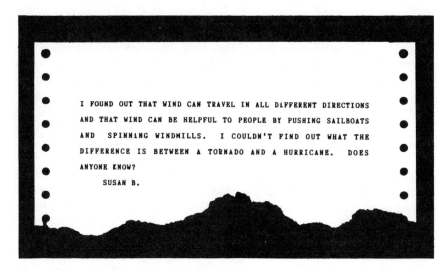

I FOUND OUT THAT WIND CAN TRAVEL IN ALL DiFFERENT DIRECTIONS
AND THAT WIND CAN BE HELPFUL TO PEOPLE BY PUSHING SAILBOATS
AND SPINNiNG WINDMILLS. I COULDN'T FIND OUT WHAT THE
DIFFERENCE IS BETWEEN A TORNADO AND A HURRICANE. DOES
ANYONE KNOW?
        SUSAN B.

Reports back to the group can be in written form.

TEACHERS' COMMUNICATIONS

Teacher-written personal communications grow from two aspects of the teachers' role. Part of the role is to trigger children's participation in written communication; this is done through teacher-written communications and through modeling of the process. At first, the teacher's messages may seem to dominate shared personal communication, but as children's familiarity with the process grows and their message writing increases, teachers deliberately reduce their public messages and move to more private communications with individuals.

In addition, just like any other member of the group, a teacher generates and responds to written communications directed to individuals or to small groups and uses them to extend the personal relationships with the learners established in other ways. Some of these messages resemble functional print a little, but when the print consists of messages directed to specific individuals, rather than to the group at large, it is part of the group's message exchange and becomes a model for continuing shared personal communication.

Triggering Children's Communications

Teacher-written messages inviting specific people to personal, individual activities give many children their first involvement in personal communication. Each invitation is addressed to a particular person and signed by the teacher, as the writer of the message. Children who find a personal invitation addressed to them one morning look carefully for messages on following mornings, and when an invitation is for something personally interesting ("Would you like to illustrate your book on horses with the new paints?") and also requests a response ("Please let me know if you would, and I'll help you set them up"), the dialogue is ready to begin. Some teachers establish a permanent personal message board near the display of daily functional print, and children look there for personal communications from the teacher each morning. Other teachers use the central message board for teacher-to-child invitations to cultivate interest in communication, but gradually phase it out in favor of a variety of locations for ongoing personal communications initiated more often by children than by adults.

Written, personally directed messages making appointments with children for conferences, planning, or other events are also used to encourage children to read the environment frequently, seeking messages addressed to them. Teachers make sure that they are seen placing many of the messages where children can find them, and they also return to the posted notes to check for responses while children are still there.

As soon as an opportunity presents itself, in the form of a posted message from a child to the teacher, written responses to children's communications begin to appear. A teacher may write a response beneath the original message, or answer with a new message, replacing the original note. Responses may be comments, answers to questions, thanks for something said, or some other statement that is directly connected to the original message. The impact of a written answer is very powerful, and sometimes provides the motivation for more written communication as children begin to write messages in order to receive replies. At first, children direct most messages to teachers, because they look forward to replies, but gradually the focus shifts away from the teacher as the center of communication to the others in the environment. Teachers encourage this by pointing out child-generated messages and responses, offering suggestions, and making supportive comments to individuals using shared written communication.

Ongoing Communications

The primary purpose for establishing shared personal communication in the environment is to engage children in the spontaneous use of literacy, but it also is genuinely useful for teachers as they work through the day with children. Written notes can't replace the sustained personal interactions or the brief exchanges between teachers and children that are part of the teaching-learning process, but they do extend the teacher's ability to touch each child in some personal way each day. Teachers write follow-up comments and questions related to particular projects or lessons ("Your idea about strengthening the roof supports should work well") and they acknowledge work they have observed, the products they have seen displayed, and the processes children used during their learning activities ("I noticed the textured paper you used to mount your drawing this morning"). Sometimes personal messages from the teacher give feedback on a child's work effort ("You really stayed focused on your writing today. Good for you") or offer specific information that may be helpful ("I think I saw an article about smallpox in last month's *Science* magazine").

Like shared personal communications written by children, teacher messages are tacked on bulletin boards, placed on the front of books stood on someone's desk, taped to the sides of cabinets, and placed beside new equipment or material that is being pointed out to individuals. When children have established the habit of writing to specific people, they begin to read everything in the environment as they look for communications addressed to themselves, so any missed messages are eventually pointed out to the right people. Teacher-written personal messages provide the initial impetus for the development of shared communication and later join with child-written messages to keep the environment alive with print that has important personal meaning to the individuals in the group.

Teacher messages can turn up anywhere.

ENVIRONMENTAL ARRANGEMENTS

The basic patterns of materials distribution and spatial organization to promote literacy are important for shared personal communication, but some special attention to provisioning, including recording tools and materials and display facilities, is very important. Written personal communication is a form of literacy for which a variety of stationery and forms are used in everyday life, and some "real" message forms or simulations can serve as models, while others remind children of previous experiences with written communication. Spatial arrangements that turn small areas into display spaces are essential to keep the flow of shared communications moving and to get messages where they can be readily found.

Recording Materials and Tools

Message Forms that are preprinted are usually designed to convey communications in abbreviated form. For example, telegraph forms and memo sheets with headings, birth announcements, telephone message slips, and dental appointment cards all contain some standard words or phrases, with blank lines for the specific information to be added. If one or two "official" models are available, simulations with headings more appropriate for the environment can be prepared, often by the children. Greeting cards contain illustrations and often, but not always, include a printed message and space for a personal note. Some commercially produced greeting cards, or illustrated notepaper that resembles them, make good models. Simulations can be made by folding large blank file cards or heavy paper, illustrating some with cut-out pictures or children's art work and leaving others blank.

Some forms are prepared by teachers to support and help shape children's social communications. Sign-on forms with space for the message and signature and lines for the individuals' signed responses are useful, as are forms for petitions. Various collection sheets with headings for names or undesignated headings are good starters for gathering opinions or asking for directory data.

Some children have home experience in using prepaid-postage post cards, and if one is available for a model, and some small file cards are marked in the upper right-hand corner with a printing stamp, a rash of personal messages result. Quite a few of these will be private, rather than posted, however, because if the model is used, the address appears on one side and the message on the other. Picture postcards, or child-made versions of them, show the message and address on the same side, but children are sometimes more interested in the picture than the message, so, again, many will become private communications, placed in mailboxes rather than posted. Still, postcards have many possibilities for shared personal communication, and their form connects them with community life, making them very attractive to children.

Papers of different shapes and sizes, smaller than the standard composition or typing paper, suggest memo and note writing very effectively. Holders just the size of the paper keep the supply available, and if a writing tool is also available, they are even more likely to stimulate written communication. Some of this raw material is prepared for the environment by teachers and children. The paper can be cut into different sizes and can be recycled by using the back. Sometimes families contribute small collections of unused stationery and notepaper and also blank envelopes of various sizes. The envelopes, when accompanied by paper and design directions for envelope making, are very attractive and much used, but more often for private communications, so teachers who wish to emphasize shared communication as a way of contributing to the print in the environment may choose to limit the areas provisioned with envelopes, and the number of envelopes available.

Variety in recording tools helps to stimulate shared communications, especially when some can be used to make illustrations. There is something attractive about a pen or pencil clipped to a holder of note slips, and children tend to return those recording tools to their clips, provided the clips are permanently attached to the paper holder. Some children enjoy watching the color flow onto the page as they write, and multicolored collections of felt-tipped pens stimulate their message writing. Others prefer pencils or dark-colored pens, and some will use any nearby recording tool.

Display Facilities

Most people try to place written notes where they think the intended reader is likely to find them. At home, notes are placed on the refrigerator, beside the front door, on the table where everybody leaves their belongings, on someone's pillow, or even on the car's dashboard. At school, a similar variety of possibilities increases the likelihood that each person will find his or her messages quickly and easily.

Central message boards for personal communications are helpful, but often part of that display space is needed for functional print, so additional, smaller spaces are needed around the environment. In

People usually return
the recording tool
to its clip.

some cases, the small display areas are parts of bulletin boards with surfaces that accept tacks or pushpins, and those display tools are made available in small containers that can be attached to the display area. Many display spaces for shared communication are made of materials that aren't intended for tacks. Metal cabinets, wooden book-cases, fabric screens, plastic dividers, desk sides, chalkboards, and pegboard surfaces need different display tools, and products are more often displayed when needed tools are nearby. Small magnets for metal cabinets and chalkboards, masking tape for smooth, unpainted sur-faces, pins for fabrics, and clips for surfaces that don't accept adhesives are just a few of the display tools that keep the messages where they can be shared.

When work spaces are located within reach of all furniture holding materials or dividing space, effective spatial organization creates many small, widely distributed display spaces. These necessary small spaces are found on unused surfaces of the furniture where people can see posted messages.

EVIDENCE OF CHILDREN'S GROWTH

It's fairly easy to recognize an environment that promotes shared personal communication within the group, by the number of individ-ual, child-generated materials that are visibly displayed. When an environment displays only teacher-generated messages or teacher-assigned writings, it's unlikely that it will foster communications through print. Where there is an active use of literacy for posted messages and replies, the materials visible within the environment offer information about children's social development, growth in ability to convey messages through print, and their awareness of events within the classroom and community.

Children's growing and changing social relationships are revealed in their messages to one another. A survey of shared communications on any school day shows who is writing to whom, what the shared interests of the writer and receiver may be, and whether or not the quality of the interaction is supportive, and constructive. Many literacy environment teachers think it's important to review shared communications frequently, in order to keep aware of the social relationships expressed through literacy and to judge when new environmental suggestions and changes of direction are needed to keep communication positive and constructive.

After the children have left for the day, there is a rich supply of information about the way children can use literacy for several different functions, but the end-of-the-day information tells much less about children's personal communication than about other uses. To obtain information about personal communication, teachers try to find time to read the environment during the day, because the short life of posted messages means that most of them have been removed by the end of the day. Children perceive personal communications as informal and tend to produce them quickly, so those products may offer the best picture of conventions and production skills that have been internalized and so can be used without inhibiting the writing process.

The content of shared communications is also very revealing, especially in the commentary messages. What events children choose to comment about, how much the knowledge content of their studies is expressed as shared interest, or how much awareness of community events is expressed gives insight into the connections children are building between their school experiences and their personal and community lives.

7

Knowledge Content and Literacy

Language and literacy acquisition are readily identified purposes for schools, because they are so visible. After all, reading, writing, speaking, and listening are things people do, and these behaviors can be seen. However, knowledge is also important as one of the school's several curriculum goals. A person's knowledge is less visible than language and literacy competence. Knowledge represents something one knows about, as opposed to knowing how to do something; so the growth of children's knowledge often receives less public attention than literacy growth.

From infancy, children's waking hours are spent investigating the world around them; they explore by reaching, touching, and moving to find out more and to understand. In some ways the process of knowledge building resembles the development of language and literacy. Children grow in language and literacy by using them, and they use them spontaneously when they see them as useful for their own purposes (Smith, 1978). Similarly, knowledge building requires the learners' active and personal involvement, and children become involved with knowledge content when they see it connected with their own basic purpose: making sense of the world (Ortiz & Loughlin, 1986).

As children encounter unfamiliar situations and information, they try to connect that information with what they already know; when it doesn't seem to make sense, they shift or accommodate their current knowledge so the new data fit, in order to add or assimilate it (Piaget, 1971), and the information is stored in the form of ideas. This is the way they build knowledge. Elementary-school children become personally involved with information encountered through firsthand experience and through materials that are literal representations of the real world. They are unlikely to build knowledge with information presented in words alone.

Teaching strategies based on this view of knowledge building begin by providing an encounter with new information that is so compelling a child wants to know more. When interest is aroused and children are ready for further exploration, activities such as observing or reading enable children to acquire additional information. The information-gathering activities are alternated with reorganizing activities such as writing or drawing, in which children use or express information while changing its form (Taba, 1968); this helps them understand and retain the knowledge.

Both information gathering and reorganizing activities are important in knowledge building. A long series of information-gathering activities with no opportunity for reorganization makes it difficult for children to make knowledge their own. It is equally difficult to reorganize without fresh information. This helps explain why sometimes after several lively sessions of journal or story writing children can't think of anything else to write about, and writing becomes a terrible labor. Writing is a reorganization activity, and writers eventually can use up their information, so these behaviors may mean that children have run out of material. Writing can be revitalized through experiences offering fresh information.

Language, literacy, and knowledge acquisition is interwoven in children's learning experiences. Language and literacy are a part of knowledge building when they are pulled into the functional contexts of gathering and sorting information and of the expression and communication of knowledge, and content provides the focus for the activity. Knowledge is central in literacy growth because the interpretation of a language text combines the intended meaning of the writer and the personal knowledge of the reader. Growth in language and literacy demands compelling content to read, write, and talk about. Growth in knowledge demands the inquiry tools provided by language and literacy. Teacher decisions about the particular knowledge content offered through provisioning are shaped by several sources. The ongoing instructional program in the subject matter areas supplies content that can be incorporated into environmental invitations for inquiry; so do important events in the community and the interests related to them. Children's interests often provide a starting place for content that then connects to the knowledge focus of the formal curriculum; the environment's content introduces, reinforces, and extends teachers' instructional programs. However, a wider range of topics and subjects is needed to meet the diverse interests of a group and to involve each in extended inquiry and literacy activity at the same time.

The strong connections between literacy activity and knowledge content have implications for arrangements in the literacy environment. Some environmentally provoked encounters, information gathering, and reorganizing activities are actually literacy activities, and accompanying literacy activity is encouraged by combinations of literacy-related provisions with a variety of information sources.

THE FROG

A few days before school began, Mrs. Driver learned that she could borrow a frog from the biology department at the university, and she arranged to keep one for several weeks. She placed the frog in its terrarium in a prominent position on a shelf where everybody would be able to see it. Above the terrarium two illustrated books about frogs stood on a narrow shelf with the cover drawings showing. Beside the terrarium she placed a chart on which she had written some specific information about the frog.

The new first graders and the returning second-grade children in her class would find the animal in its temporary habitat on their first morning, and she was sure the frog's activity would catch their attention. She knew that these children and their older brothers or sisters often found frogs beside the community's irrigation ditches at this time of year, and the children would know something about them.

It didn't take long for the children to notice the frog. Some asked the teacher about it, a couple of the older children began to read the information on the chart, and several others said they had seen a middle-school neighbor with a much bigger frog from the ditch bank. Somebody announced, "Frogs are fish," but several disagreed, because frogs came out of the water and moved along the banks. Mrs. Driver noticed two or three children leafing through books they had taken down from the shelf above the terrarium, and one child read captions aloud for the others. More than half of the children had immediately accepted the invitation to find out about frogs, and their discussion was drawing in others. Later, in a group meeting, someone asked, "Are we going to do frogs?" and the teacher responded that there was more information available in the classroom and in the school library for those who were interested and made a note to herself to investigate filmstrips and videotapes.

Later, as she reviewed the day, Mrs. Driver decided not to present the topic of frogs as a study focus for the whole class, but to support it environmentally and let it run its course as self-initiated activity, keeping other content possibilities available and supported at the same time. Over a week's time she added more information sources to the arrangement. A filmstrip, more informational books, a life-cycle chart borrowed from the middle school, and a few vocabulary cards (cold-blooded, warm-blooded, hibernate, amphibian, moist, carnivorous, tadpoles, lung) were gradually added. In several brief exchanges with the frog scholars, she helped them locate material in an encyclopedia, read a page aloud for them, listened to children tell what they had just found out. Later, on request, she read one of the informational books to the whole class.

Many children were now involved with print because of their interest in the frog, but few were doing any writing, which the teacher wanted to encourage. Except for the vocabulary cards, there wasn't any suggestion or support for writing in the present arrangement. That was remedied by pushing a single desk and chair against the cabinet where the frog was kept; placing a holder with pencils, crayons, and writing paper on it; and putting a roll of masking tape beneath a new sign that said "Frog Observations." During the day several children asked about the sign, and the teacher read it aloud for them. When someone asked what the masking tape was for, she explained it was to fasten their work to the wall.

In a day or two, Mrs. Driver noticed that two children sat at the desk in front of the terrarium during a work session, watching the frog carefully, and discussing it intently. The next morning, during the writing period, they sat together again and began to write. They consulted about spellings and occasionally asked someone to spell particular words; they collaborated on the writing, decided how to illustrate their paper, and finally, after two days of work, hung their "Frog Observation" on the wall. They had used their best phonetic judgment about spelling, concentrating mainly on finding a way to report their observations on paper. Within a few days, other children had picked up on the idea and had posted their own observation notes.

The teacher enjoyed watching the children at work, which gave her information about their growth and attitudes toward learning. The environment supported some very serious self-directed learning, even this early in the school year, and she knew that other additions to the frog arrangement could stimulate the inquiry of others who were ready to become involved. She also saw ways to build on that work as she developed plans for the science unit that would soon begin.

INVITATIONS

In literacy classrooms there is a variety of vivid print and nonprint information sources that invite investigation. The initial invitation comes from interesting objects and materials, and it is extended by more detailed information in the accompanying print. Sometimes these invitations are arranged by children, but more often they are arranged by the teacher to encourage long-term involvement with knowledge and print in integrated activities.

Capturing Interest

Teachers who arrange invitations for investigation begin by choosing objects and materials that focus the invitations. Selection of those materials establishes the knowledge content of the environment. Elementary-school children express their interests in concrete terms; they are more interested in things than ideas, so the information sources that initially attract them are real, such as natural specimens and cultural artifacts, or they are literal representations of reality, such as models and pictures. The content decisions for arranged invitations are somewhat different from content decisions for teacher-designed learning experiences. Environmental arrangements must function alone, without teacher introduction or explanation. The content of the environment first engages children in self-directed inquiry, and then may lead toward connections with the instructional content of the curriculum. Environmental content is most effective when related to children's interests and past experiences (Van Dongen, 1983), or events in their community (Martin, 1982), and when it can be presented through concrete objects and literal representations, displayed for access and self-initiated use.

These content invitations begin with an information source that displays its data clearly, usually in nonprint form; illustrated materials with small amounts of print are useful. Materials from the natural environment are inherently interesting, and children provide many interesting specimens, from unfamiliar insects found on the way to school to organized collections displayed by older children. Teachers build on those interests by displaying living creatures that will change or become active, natural specimens that can be handled and examined, or other concrete information sources. X-ray photographs, satellite infrared photo maps, anatomical models of the human eye, and forest service posters of birds and plants of a region are information sources that match children's interest by offering literal representations of the natural world.

Content about the social world makes connections too, as children broaden their understanding of their society. Realia, like clothing and tools, engage children's attention. Historical records, diagrams, and familiar household equipment represent the social world in interesting ways.

Print and nonprint materials from the community have special meaning and high interest for children, whether the materials represent the community as the children now perceive it or reflect views of the community from different perspectives or times. Photographic records of change in the community (Loughlin, 1976), materials sent outside the community to encourage tourism, or markedly different picture views of familiar areas quickly stimulate interest. Contemporary and historical documents have an interesting appearance because of the forms, seals, and signatures that mark them as official, and souvenirs of community celebrations and fairs, or clothing and farming implements from the community's past, touch children's past experience and draw them to the content.

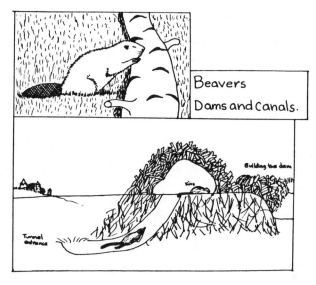

Children are interested in the natural world.

Invitations to Print

After interest-capturing information sources have been arranged, other materials are added to invite children to the use of print and books. The invitations to print are either direct, when the print is about the objects or information, or they are indirect, in functional print that helps organize children's use of the objects. Direct invitations such as titles and labels identify displayed objects, or explain where they came from. Indirect invitations, such as displayed directions for the use of unfamiliar equipment, inform children about procedures, and sign-ons help everybody get a chance to use especially attractive equipment.

Books become part of the invitations when one or two, related to the nonprint information sources, are displayed close by. Of course unless the relationship is clear to the children when they first see the books, they can miss the invitation to use the print form of the content. Illustrations on the book cover, titles in bold print, a reference book with a marker at related information, or an informational book opened to pertinent illustrations make the connections clearer and draw children to the print. It isn't necessary for these books to contain all possible information, since they are functioning here as part of the invitation to investigate; clear connection to the content is enough, merely conveying that there is more to be known, and further information is available.

GATHERING INFORMATION

A person interested in an invitational display of objects and print can find suggestions nearby for more extensive information gathering and use available provisions to support those research activities. Sometimes information gathering occurs through literacy activity, and at other times it involves processes that aren't in themselves literacy, although they can reasonably be accompanied by literacy activity.

Literacy Activities

Support for literacy activities in data gathering is established primarily through provisioning, rather than materials arangement. When the stimulus for investigation is already present and children move to gather additional information from print, their literacy activities are elicited by the characteristics of detailed information sources. A variety of materials, presenting relevant information in print and other symbols, encourages interested children to search further.

Reading informational books, single-copy textbooks, and reference books is a straightforward way for children to find information; biographies and fictional trade books with settings related to the topic immerse readers in relevant events and settings. Books and pamphlets from associations and government agencies, magazine articles, and teacher-made summaries of information help to expand the books and print information useful for children's inquiry.

Consulting written files, labeled-picture files, and computer files call for the use of literacy as children locate the information stored in the file and as they read or interpret it. Children sometimes find information in clippings or documents that are part of community records; personal documents from community members are also of great interest. Such information sources within the environment support children in their search and sometimes encourage them to extend the search to other locations. Community offices, archives, and the local newspaper morgue provide important materials to be brought back to show others. Some types of information can be gathered by reading diagrams and drawings, in which nonprint symbols such as lines, boxes, arrows, and other symbols present relationships between the elements. Whether the print is a central source of information or simply labels parts of the diagram, a child must read in order to interpret the print. Blueprints, wiring diagrams, directions for assembling furniture shipped in pieces, and sewing-pattern direction sheets are diagrams children can read when objects or constructions they represent can also be seen. Maps, flow charts, family trees, and organizational diagrams also offer very useful literacy information.

Connecting Information and Literacy

Interviewing, observing, experimenting, and viewing or listening to films or tapes are effective forms of information gathering that don't necessarily require literacy. The significant information is not offered through print in these activities, and literacy isn't directly elicited by the characteristics of particular information sources. They are important forms of information gathering, however, and often planned in content subject programs, with the assumption that they are the focus of teacher-designed learning activities. Within the literacy environment, self-initiated use of these data-gathering processes, coupled with literacy, is then encouraged, as it extends and reinforces the teacher-

CARDBOARD PERISCOPE

Christine Coleman

These plans are for use with two 3 1/2" x 2" lady's rectangular pocket mirrors. The size of your periscope will naturally vary according to the size of the mirrors used.

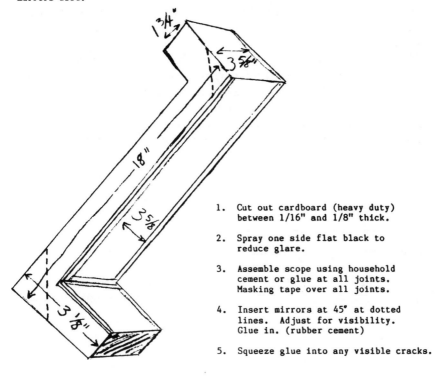

1. Cut out cardboard (heavy duty) between 1/16" and 1/8" thick.

2. Spray one side flat black to reduce glare.

3. Assemble scope using household cement or glue at all joints. Masking tape over all joints.

4. Insert mirrors at 45° at dotted lines. Adjust for visibility. Glue in. (rubber cement)

5. Squeeze glue into any visible cracks.

Diagrams require reading of words and other symbols.

initiated program. The stimulus and support for the activities and accompanying literacy is offered primarily through materials arrangement. Literacy provisions already present are arranged with the information sources and teacher-prepared print that encourages data gathering.

For instance, teachers who wish to encourage experimentation combine raw materials or specimens with tools and materials that might be used in an experiment and may display a question or two that could be investigated. Additional provisions in the area encourage the use of literacy during the experiment. Displayed directions for two or three experiments, or directions for the use of a stopwatch or a microscope, help children organize the experiment. A sign-on chart inviting signed hypotheses about outcomes, notepaper and recording tools, references, forms for recording procedures and findings, and tools and materials to store information for later reorganization all focus on the experiment and its findings and present very strong suggestions for literacy activity.

Carefully arranged suggestions in the environment encourage some children to initiate interviewing as an information-gathering experience. Sometimes a clipping of a newspaper interview, a teacher-written question, or a sign-on to gather suggestions can get children started, as they begin to think about people who might share relevant information. More literacy activity is encouraged by notepads and

Name _____	
Type of Food _____	
Day 1 Observation (Wednesday)	Day 2 Observation
Day 3 Observation	Day 6 Observation

Record forms connect literacy to experiments.

recording tools, list paper or simple forms for planning interview questions, a tape recorder with operating directions, materials and tools for reporting, and display facilities for sharing the information gathered.

Because modern equipment for viewing or listening to films and tapes is easily operated, children are able to use these tools independently. Films, filmstrips, and audio- or videotapes are good information sources for elementary-school children; the information they offer is representational and is also very concentrated. The use of films or tapes for information gathering is stimulated by materials arrangement when they are displayed with labels visible and close to related information sources. Since the information on film or tape is presented visually or with sound rather than with print, additional materials encourage literacy activity. Displayed directions for operating machines help children get started. Note-taking materials, lists of study questions attached to the film or tape, displayed directions for discussing and summarizing a film, recording tools and materials for written reviews, and display space for them are prominently displayed to urge further use of literacy.

Direct observation is a data-gathering activity that fascinates children. Observing is suggested by arrangements focusing visual attention on something that changes over time. Animals, plant growth, construction projects in the classroom and outside, weather, and human behavior are good examples. If the subjects under observation can be moved, they are placed in areas that also hold tools for observing and viewing, like cages and magnifying glasses. There are times when a window is the best viewing tool for a subject external to the classroom, such as clouds, weather, or fledgling birds nesting in a tree. In that case, observations are stimulated by books, charts, or other information near the window, and brief print labels or questions to help focus attention. Other literacy components effective for observation arrangements include displayed directions for observation procedures, references, forms for observation data, and tools and materials for note taking, planning, and reporting.

REORGANIZING INFORMATION

Reorganization activities, in which children take the information they have gathered and express it in a different form, help them integrate new information. Some, like writing and charting, are literacy activities, and others, like mural painting or dramatizing, are not, but can be

Information-Gathering Activities

Through Literacy
Reading Books
Consulting Files
Interpreting Diagrams and Drawings

Associated with Literacy
Interviewing
Observing
Experimenting
Viewing or Listening to Films and Tapes

accompanied by literacy. All involve some product, which may be as short lived as a dramatization or a small group discussion, or longer lasting, such as a written play or a permanent construction. Arrangements to suggest reorganization of information are presented alongside the materials encouraging information gathering. Sometimes the presence of displayed products of other people's reorganization activity or just the opportunity to become involved in one of the activities instigates an information search.

Literacy Activities for Reorganization

Report writing is one way for children to analyze and express their understanding of the information and ideas they have been working with; creative writing is another. Models of possibilities, such as articles, reports, biographies, diaries, short histories, and poetry, help chidren consider ways to reorganize and sometimes support the previous stage of information gathering at the same time. Recording tools and materials, illustrating and book-binding materials, and a good supply of references enable children to proceed with these writing and reorganizing activities.

Charting is an interesting activity in which children arrange information in some way that shows relationships. Young children may do this through classifying, then building a chart by arranging cut-out illustrations, by drawing, or by writing lists. Written titles and captions are part of that charting. Older children may produce more sophisticated charts, reflecting more mature analyses and thinking processes, in which print plays a more central role. Chart making is stimulated by models, planning forms, or written questions posed by the teacher. Access to the displayed interview reports, observation records, and other information from data-gathering activities support analysis and chart designing and may also provide the impetus for charting. References, chart paper, notepaper, recording tools, and old magazines with scissors arranged near the models also support the process. Display space for the completed charts makes it possible for them to serve as style models for children reorganizing different sets of information.

Activities Accompanied by Literacy

Construction is an activity that has strong attraction and holding power for children of all ages (Sutton-Smith, 1968), and it is extremely useful as a reorganization experience. Dioramas, models, simple machines, or sets and props to accompany dramatizations call upon accurate information as they are planned and built. The major stimu-

Children use charts to show relationships.

lus is the presence of construction materials and tools. Models, pictures, diagrams, drawings, and illustrated references support planning. List paper for materials and dimensions, graph paper for drawing plans, recording materials and tools, displayed directions for the use of tools, three-dimensional display spaces, paper and sentence strips for labeling displays, and books about construction add literacy dimensions. These markedly increase the likelihood that children will make use of literacy during the construction activity.

Illustrating enables children to visually represent knowledge they find difficult to put into writing. Young children may find it easier to draw than write about something; they can review and synthesize information as they draw and then follow up with some writing. Older students present details through illustration, as an elaboration of a written text. Murals, large-sized group illustrations, are complex projects that involve group analysis and planning as well as shared work. Analysis of the pooled information of the group and planning how to represent it pictorially provides the reorganization experience. Intermediate-grade children are more likely to initiate group murals independently than are primary-school children. Probably mural paper, space enough to use it, and a display space offer sufficient stimulus for this activity, but the raw materials and tools that support illustrating, and relevant information in the form of pictures, photos, or child-made illustrations, are also effective. Literacy is added to all illustrating activities through recording tools, planning materials, list paper, references, and display labels. Planning sign-ons are functional literacy additions for mural making.

Child-initiated focused small-group discussions tend to occur mainly in classrooms where focused discussions are also part of teacher-planned learning activities and when the settings for them are carefully arranged. Spatial organization placing objects of interest within a circular seating arrangement tends to generate talk about the materials in the center. The literacy connection comes through sign-on appointment charts for getting together, a displayed copy of agreed-upon rules for discussion, notepaper, larger paper for discussion summaries, chart paper for possible relationship charts, a variety of recording tools, and display facilities.

Role playing and dramatizing are natural activities for most children, and are also effective ways of reorganizing knowledge. Teachers often arrange settings to encourage dramatization and may also provide some arrangements to enable children who wish to share their dramatizations with others to present performances. However, the value of dramatizing for children's knowledge building is in the planning and acting out, rather than in performance for an audience (Moffett, 1973). Encouragement for the activity comes from expressing and communicating tools such as costumes or puppets near the materials used in the information-gathering process. Raw materials for making costumes, scenery, props, or puppets also offer strong suggestions. The dramatizing activity is likely to include literacy if the area provides tools and materials for planning or script writing, models of scripts and staging directions, illustrated references, and displayed directions for making puppets or costumes.

Reorganization Activities

Through Literacy
Report writing
Creative writing
Charting

Associated with Literacy
Constructing
Illustrating
Making murals
Dramatizing

TEACHERS' ENVIRONMENTAL WORK

Behind-the-scenes work for teachers as they arrange the knowledge content of the environment includes special provisioning efforts, materials arrangement, and preparation of displayed print. During the day, as children use the environment and its resources, teachers model the inquiry process and support children's efforts through brief interactions with individuals and groups.

Provisioning and Arranging

Teachers provision for the content of literacy with a special focus on information sources; the richer the information offered to children for their self-initiated exploration, the more elaborate and extensive their involvement with literacy. Teachers expand the standard school provisioning by searching for a variety of materials to increase the information potential of the environment, and they discover that finding, selecting, and acquiring information sources is both challenging and satisfying. The process has been described in detail elsewhere (Loughlin & Suina, 1982), so only a few major points are reviewed here.

Formal instructional materials aren't sufficient to support self-initiated study of content and literacy, because the breadth of interests pursued by active children consumes a much wider variety of information than textbooks alone can offer. A variety of forms in which the information is offered is also important because different forms of information (displayed or stored) play different roles in inquiry and because within a group of children there are varying levels of ability to retrieve information from print and nonprint forms.

The community provides the majority of information sources, which are available sometimes as loaned materials, as give-aways, as scrounged and recycled materials, and as discoveries from the natural environment. Sharing and trading materials between classrooms is common, and many teachers share both the search and the information sources.

Provisioning for content is never finished. Interests and activities change, and new content and invitations are needed to keep children involved. Some content strands may continue to appear, but the specific provisions that stimulate and support children's study change, attracting different children and pulling others back to familiar content in more sophisticated ways. Teachers who provision will seem to be on the lookout for information sources wherever they go, and their ability to recognize the information potential of very simple materials and objects is the key to environmental content that involves children in knowledge building and literacy.

Arranging materials to emphasize the content possibilities of provisions is another behind-the-scenes task that is never finished. Each day, after noting children's interests and work processes, teachers add information sources, put out different recording tools, remove materials that have run their course, or relocate materials for better access. As children progress in their work, the reorganization of materials already in the environment highlights suggestions, leading them on to next steps.

Teacher-prepared print is important in activating the knowledge content of the literacy environment, but it is extremely brief, never replacing or overshadowing the other provisions. Sometimes teachers offer information not available in other print sources, and they pose provocative questions, issue invitations, or provide directions for equipment use. The print and material displays work together to clarify activity possibilities and support children in their work.

During the Day

There are many moments during the day when teachers model, listen, comment, and encourage as children work in the environment. These exchanges are ways of activating the content potential of the environment, helping children approach and think about the displayed information, and encouraging next steps in inquiry. A teacher may pick up a magnifying glass and use it to examine a natural specimen, or leaf through a book to compare a specimen with illustrations. Teachers briefly model the use of other tools or recording procedures in a natural way, making notes, adding to a graph, experimenting with a balance scale. These moments of teachers' modeling remind some children that provisions can be used, inform others how they are used, and provide the impetus for yet others to become involved in the first steps of inquiry.

Almost without exception, children are eager to tell someone about their activities, and frequently it is the teacher, passing by, who is available. The teacher takes a moment to listen and responds with a quick comment acknowledging a child's plan, achievement, or discovery. The brief moment of listening and responding is a powerful motivation and support for children in their knowledge building.

ENVIRONMENTAL EVIDENCE OF GROWTH

Children produce a variety of materials in their information-gathering and reorganization activities; many are displayed, others arranged within some container as work-in-progress. These materials are good sources of insight about children's growth in literacy, because in each case they show which individuals can use literacy independently and which literacy behaviors they use. Independent use is a good indication of the internalization of acquired behaviors. Teachers learn how individuals interpret information from print by noting accuracy of notes, captions, or illustrations in their displays. Knowing the specific information sources available, they gather further information about the level at which individuals function independently. The products of reorganization activities reveal progression in children's growing knowledge, and just as much about their uses of literacy to express and communicate that knowledge. In the written products children show their capacity to use print for their own purposes.

Observing

Teachers catch glimpses and overhear snatches of conversation as they move through the environment; other information comes from brief exchanges with children during the day. They note which children are asking for help in reading information and who is helping. They hear consultations about spelling and other writing conventions; they watch collaborative reorganization efforts evolve, noting how the literacy tasks are divided; they see which print resources, at which levels, are chosen by individuals for their information gathering. Teachers are alert to any brief bits of information that can expand their insight into children's independent uses of literacy and at the same time help them understand the growth of individuals in the knowledge-building process.

8

Writing

The ability to write clearly is a significant long-term goal for any literacy curriculum, and this widely accepted goal is a popular target for many of the criticisms of schooling that appear in newspapers and other media today (Boyer, 1983). Extensive attention in professional journals to the development of writing and instructional approaches to teaching writing also reflects the importance of the writing process as part of a literacy curriculum (DeFord, 1980).

Some children actually begin to write by age three; and the successful efforts of some nursery-school children in composing messages or statements have been described by several researchers (Read, 1975). They show that young children who frequently see adults writing understand that print represents language and ideas, and these children may begin to write long before entering school, as they explore the uses and conventions of print. Children's early writings are not accurate according to adult standards for form and spelling, and much of children's energy is devoted to finding out how to present words, but they also engage in earnest and often successful efforts to compose messages and statements phonetically. As they find out more about letters and the sounds of letters, children who are involved in "invented writing" incorporate that information into their written messages, gradually using closer approximations to standard print conventions in word placement, letter form, spelling, and simple sentence punctuation as they continue to write. Teachers working with seven- and eight-year-olds who have gained control of manuscript writing and basic print conventions often observe the determination with which the older children move to cursive writing and add more punctuation conventions, such as quotation marks, to their work. The incorporation of more mature print conventions at this time seems to be extremely satisfying and is accompanied by increasing self-directed editing.

Writing, like other forms of spontaneous literacy activity in the elementary school, frequently takes place in a social setting (King, 1982). Children consult one another, finding models and resources for conventions and sharing their skills. They formulate stories by telling them to somebody, and they rehearse possible phrasings or word choices orally as they try them out on a listener, then move into writing.

People write for many reasons, and, whether they are telling stories, expressing strongly held views, reporting events, or explaining relationships, it is a creative activity. Creativity is reflected in the ordering of thoughts, perceptions, and language to express the ideas and structures of their individual views of the world (Golub, 1975). Materials and events that stimulate people to write are as varied as the writers and their backgrounds. Children are stimulated by stories they have heard, objects that trigger memories, shared experiences, apparatus they can manipulate, books they have enjoyed, animals they observe. The commitment to writing has different sources for different writers (Egan, 1981, November), so varied stimuli are needed.

There are many instructional approaches for teaching children to write; these are well represented in educational literature and are not presented here. This discussion focuses on the environment's potential contribution to children's growth as it offers purpose and opportunity to develop competence in print conventions and become deeply involved in writing.

Writing centers are often set up in elementary-school classrooms, but they are not the answer to children's need for literate surroundings that generate the content of writing and offer references for the conventions of print. The widespread distribution of tools and materials, with something interesting to read and write about, offers constant encounters with print and continuous suggestions for writing. Stimulation for children's creative writing exists in all parts of the environ-

Writing takes place in a social setting.

ment, in both the provisioning and the arrangement of materials. Social settings where children can talk about writing and share knowledge, display spaces where children share their writing, and materials and time for feedback from readers enable children to support one another's efforts and encourage continued growth.

THE WRITING MORNING

One afternoon Mrs. Jeremiah was trying to think of ways to encourage more spontaneous writing in her primary classroom. She looked around carefully, trying to identify any provisioning problem that might keep children from choosing to write. There were recording tools and materials for everyone: individual spiral notebooks, an ample supply of writing paper, blank paper, blank books, crayons, pens, markers, and pencils in the writing area. Picture dictionaries were stored beneath the word lists on the nearby bulletin board.

As she was putting things away in the work spaces, she noticed that three areas, where the children weren't initiating writing, were without writing materials. Although free to move to find any provisions needed, children who settled in the unprovisioned areas weren't doing so. Mrs. Jeremiah decided to concentrate on materials, to see if a new arrangement would help. She removed the writing area label and distributed all but a few of the recording materials around the room. Now every area presented a variety of literacy provisions. She distributed the dictionaries around the environment and revised the next day's schedule, planning a large time block for writing in the afternoon, when she could watch the children working.

As she was looking over the room before school the next morning, Mrs. Jeremiah realized that children had produced most of their self-initiated writing in the provisioned areas that had both provisions and display facilities. During the last few moments before the children came, she placed some masking tape in the areas without bulletin boards and fastened labels saying "Display Area for Writing" to some empty surfaces where it was appropriate to use tape.

Early in the morning, four separate groups of children formed, all chatting as they worked, each in a different location. Most were recording observations of a food experiment, and a number of illustrations were made with the markers and crayons in each area.

One of the boys wrote carefully for several minutes, then put his pencil back into the basket on the table. "Look," he said, "I wrote all this stuff about my lettuce!" and read it aloud while everyone at the table listened. Another child working at the same table put her observation sheet with his in a folder on the table and held up a spiral notebook, announcing that she was going to do some writing. She opened the notebook and began to read aloud the last story she had written, while the boy listened. The two children exchanged notebooks and discussed them quietly for a few moments, then the girl picked up a marking pen and turned the page. Mrs. Jeremiah noticed the preparations for writing as she passed the area and congratulated the children on getting started.

Soon two children approached the teacher to ask for spellings of words, so Mrs. Jeremiah wrote each word at the top of a blank file card. The children placed the cards near their writing notebooks, so they could copy the words.

Around the room most of the children were writing now. The boys in a group on the carpet were talking out stories bit by bit as the composing process progressed, whether or not anyone listened. Occasionally someone responded with a comment or a laugh. Some were illustrating as they composed, others just talked it through, writing a bit, then talking about it some more, sharing thoughts and intentions with one another.

Two of the boys caught the teacher's attention as she passed by, showing her their writing and telling her about it. A few other children were writing menus for the restaurant they had arranged in the loft. One girl held her menu up to the teacher, saying that each item cost two cents. The teacher commented on the prices and the menu, while children nearby smiled, licked their lips, or made appreciative noises.

Shortly afterward, three people, consulting about the spelling of *restaurant*, remembered they had seen the word in a book. One hurried to the book rack and found it, and the three huddled over the book, turning pages until they found the word. Someone copied it on a slip of paper and handed it to another child who wrote it on the menu. As they continued, the children wanted more spellings. One looked carefully over a large nutrition chart across the room where there were labeled pictures of foods. She searched for words, and when she found a needed one, she wrote it on a slip of paper from a supply holder in the area, then delivered it to the others, who kept writing. The children commented about the foods they were listing: "Yummmm!" and "My best favorite snack!" Sometimes the word searcher found a word and slowly wrote one letter at a time, looking back for each new letter; once in a while she wrote a complete word quickly. Soon, one menu was taped on the side of the loft/restaurant, and a second one was being tacked on a bulletin board used for news items.

Now everybody in the environment was involved with some writing without any teacher assignments. According to the teacher's plan, it was time to move the children into activities, but she decided not to interrupt them; they were already thinking and composing, which she had planned for later in the day. They were using the variety of recording materials Mrs. Jeremiah had placed in the areas and had begun to display what they had written in some new locations. The dictionaries had not been used yet, but a very large and highly visible nutrition information source had been used as a reference, and the content of some writing may have been shaped by this dominant reference.

The children sustained their writing activity most of the morning. Shortly before the early lunch hour, Mrs. Jeremiah heard one of the boys say, "I'm tired of going back and forth to spell. I wish somebody would just *tell* me!" But he kept right on writing and going back and forth.

CONVENTIONS OF PRINT

The environment's role in the children's increasing competence in the use of conventions is primarily one of support. References, display facilities, and spaces for collaborative proofreading and editing offer basic support for children's growth from their early struggles to get messages into print as they begin school to the development of drafting, multiple editing, and final copy production with accurate use of conventions.

Letter Form

Alphabet cards are the most prominent references for letter form in almost every elementary-school classroom. For beginners, these are more useful when fastened to a wall *below* a chalkboard, where they can be easily seen and touched, than far above eye level over the chalkboard. Children are supported in learning letter form when the reference clearly presents the upper- and lower-case forms and the placement of letters in relation to a base line. Older children need frequent access to letter-form references as they move from manuscript to cursive writing and will need to have the new alphabet cards within reach. A grouping of alphabet models in chart form displayed within their reach is often even more versatile than the single-line display that supports the beginner.

Observations in literacy environments show that children use any displayed print as a reference if it gives needed information about letters or words, so teacher-written print is an important model. Teachers' writing demonstrates the same manuscript form that children are learning, so a high proportion of teacher-written display is appropriate. As children move into cursive writing, teacher-written segments, originally designed for other purposes, serve well as letter-form references.

Placement Conventions

Beginners' concerns about placement of writing include some basic conventions, such as where to begin, or where to put the next letters when a line is full before the word is finished. Provisioning for writing offers children support if writing paper is marked with a small symbol, such as a red dot, at the left of each line and a slightly different symbol at the top left corner of the page (Clay, 1975). As children outgrow the need for such direct individual support, teachers who are conscious of their own displayed writing as references for conventions continue to offer models such as schedules written from left to right, rather than in list form, and sentences that are longer than a single line of print.

Older children become interested in special placement conventions for writing, such as indenting paragraphs or writing business and personal letters, outlines, and scripts. References in the form of traditional charts with rules for format help some children; others make better use of teacher-written models and samples of particular forms.

Punctuation

As children gain writing competence, their needs for punctuation conventions become more complex, in part reflecting the demands of curriculum and in part keeping pace with the greater complexity of the knowledge and language at their command. Commercial charts listing rules and examples for punctuation may be useful for instructional sessions, but children tend to make more use of models. Functional print, teacher-written information sources, sentence labels, and teacher communications are good models. More permanent teacher-made charts presenting punctuation conventions in examples that visually highlight the punctuation are effective references for older children when the charts focus on a particular point.

Spelling

Spelling is a special convention of print for which awareness develops early, but gaining control over spelling is a very long process. Observations of early primary-school children looking around an environment, almost desperately, for assistance with spelling are a good indication of their awareness. They use calendars, announcements, other children's writings, teacher charts, book covers, or any other displayed print almost as much as they use word lists, dictionaries, and word banks. As their spelling vocabulary increases, children are better able to take the time to use book references, but specialized vocabulary lists related to particular content are still extremely useful.

Spelling references wherever children work are important to support their growth. Dictionaries distributed around the environment, alphabetized pocket chart word banks, personal dictionaries, such as booklets and file boxes to record new words under the proper letter, or individual word cards assembled on a large ring all support appropriate use of conventions of spelling as children write and proofread.

One of the strengths of personal dictionaries, in which children enter the words they have searched out, is that children's choices reflect both individual vocabulary preferences and the specific topics about which they write, so each dictionary is a unique fit for its collector. They provide a much larger pool of information than if each child had identical word lists.

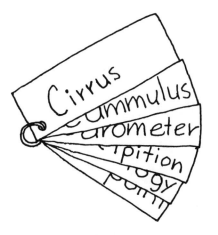

Personal dictionaries reflect individual interests.

Proofreading

Proofreading, or reviewing written materials for accuracy in the use of conventions to the extent that children are familiar with them, is a cooperative task in most literacy environments. Provisioning that offers work spaces where two children can concentrate, a variety of resources for spelling, and models for punctuation enable children to help one another in their proofreading efforts. This makes regular review a normal part of the writing process. Young children's proofreading may focus on only one or two conventions at a time, reflecting recently acquired knowledge or current interest. Older children proofread to catch detailed convention oversights and errors that occur in early drafts, but may not yet attend to editing of style or wording.

In some classrooms with computer word-processing software available for children's writing, there are spelling check programs that older elementary-school children can use for proofreading. Some programs only identify possible misspellings, treating them as typographical errors, which writers must then correct by applying their own knowledge of spelling conventions.

THE WRITING PROCESS

When children's writing grows out of their own wishes to express ideas and feelings or share important events in their lives, their involvement in the writing process is intense and personal. Provisioning

Word processing programs may proofread for spelling.

supports that process by triggering specific ideas to focus the writing and by supporting children as they develop those ideas and express them in print within the framework of accepted conventions.

Starters

Traditionally, teachers have provided story starters for children in many forms, such as phrases, titles, ideas, or beginning sentences, to help children think of something to write, but in the literacy environment these aren't necessary. The environment itself provides the "starter" for writing. Provisions stimulate ideas and feelings, support explorations, suggest projects and products, which in turn lead to writing. Writing broadly supported in this way represents children's genuine interests and concerns, which in turn build commitment to the writing process.

The impetus for children's stories comes from provisions that also serve other purposes in the environment. Young children sometimes write about the characters and events in favorite books, extending a story within the same form, or they write about the book in their own words or in another literary style. Films and filmstrips sometimes stimulate the same kind of writing, as children extend their experiences with literature.

Young children write about favorite stories.

A variety of pictures and illustrations distributed through the environment often helps children generate ideas for stories. Pictures of familiar experiences, photographs of situations that evoke strong feelings, illustrations of humorous or novel situations, and pictures of things in the community or children's homes and families can remind children of past experiences and offer topics for written narratives.

Ideas for stories also come from objects and materials in the environment. Familiar objects offering new views or perceptions of size, such as a collection of pulleys in a variety of sizes from huge to miniature, prompt some children to write Gulliver-like stories; many other novel versions of familiar equipment or materials are equally provocative. Objects and materials from home can make connections with some of the universal experiences of children within families, a focus for many of the stories children create.

When children are ready to write poems, a variety of materials support these beginnings. Some evoke vivid memories, feelings, and images from past experiences, and it is these images that help children move to writing in the forms of poetry. Souvenirs, art reproductions, illustrated books, photographs, and objects associated with personally important events generate the images that may become central themes in children's poetry. A variety of poetry in the environment's book collection provides experiences with the ideas, moods, and forms that make poetry a special form of writing. These are posted and read aloud to provide children with a growing familiarity with that form.

The visual appearance of poetry in print is an important characteristic that may interest some children in writing poetry. Displays of print graphics in posters or opened books, teacher-prepared models of poetry in varied visual forms, or displays of poetry written with calligraphy tools help those children begin. Others may be more interested in the sounds and rhythms of poetry, and their explorations can be supported by tape recorders used for reading and recording their own poems or those of others. Poetry on records or tapes offers a variety of forms and rhythms, and soft rhythmic instruments sometimes enable children to explore the rhythms of poetry in a direct way as they accompany the oral models or their own readings.

Play writing is stimulated by a setting for drama, and the plots or themes may at first reflect those of familiar literature. Trade books, children's written stories, or filmstrip versions of children's books often provide beginnings for play writing. Older children draw on familiar stories or real-life events or drama from film, television, or theater experiences. Drama-related materials, such as puppets, props, or a stage, are often enough to stimulate the development of a new play. Models of scripts may stimulate ideas about drama for older children, and availability of resources for production supports the completion of the writing process.

The desire to express opinions or strongly held feelings in arguments and persuasions or to clarify burning issues offers a strong impetus for writing (Moffett, 1973). Some of the need for such writing comes from living together in the classroom, especially with young children; others are connected with ongoing questions in a larger social context of the children's school, community, or society. The decision to deal with these themes can be stimulated through materials such as clippings from magazines and newspapers, newsletters from the school or the group, displayed records of events, or objects and pictures related to important questions and issues. Some of the stimulus for writing about burning issues is indirect, as the environment provokes activities and events from which the issues grow.

Informational reports grow out of children's encounters with the knowledge content of the environment, as described in a previous chapter, and are stimulated by both print and nonprint information sources. Living plants and creatures; examples of physical phenomena, maps, globes and other representations of the social world; and

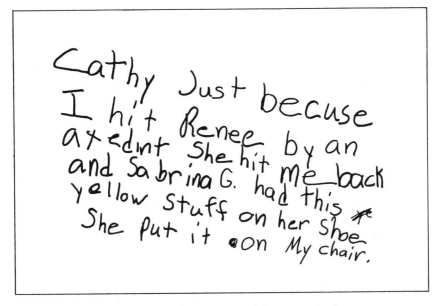

Burning issues may be reported from a day's events.

various illustrations of the natural and social world offer invitations to become involved with information and support children through their inquiry to the final stage of organizing their knowledge into written form.

Encouraging Extension

After children become involved in self-initiated writing, the process is sustained through arrangements that encourage collaborating, trying out ideas, talking with others, sharing and receiving feedback, editing and illustrating their work.

Collaboration is supported by spatial organization offering sheltered work spaces where two or three people can talk without intrusion. In these work spaces, discussions in which children talk out their intentions, plan stories or reports, or engage in multiple authorship are important as children develop their ideas and put them into writing. Print information sources and references in the sheltered work spaces enable children to verify information and conventions as they compose, and some basic provisions for the writing collaboration, such as notepaper and draft paper, writing tools, and folders, envelopes, or other containers for the work-in-progress, support children's continued efforts.

Children frequently try out their ideas for plot or phrasing as they write, telling somebody what they are about to say, or talking about events in their narratives to see how they sound. For young children this is an important part of the writing process and can be supported by work spaces organized to shelter a small group of children in a social setting. Some arrangements encourage a brief tryout of print versions of an idea or story. A chalkboard makes it possible to try out and change print very easily, as do most computer word-processing programs. Plenty of recycled scratch paper, which conveys its expendability by its abundance, is another way to support trying out phrases and other portions of a person's writing.

Children seem to need to try out their ideas when writing plays. They act out a scene they have talked over as a way of thinking through dialogue or plot. Sometimes they try out only the words; at other times they may need to act out physically some of the events they are considering. Insulated work spaces for small groups, tape recorders that can be used to record intended dialogue for a play, and plenty of notepaper and draft paper support these efforts.

Children who write poetry also benefit by trying out their work as it develops. Facilities to record and listen to their own poetry replayed are very useful. Individual and small-group work spaces are important, so the writers have the option of working in a social setting or trying out their work in privacy.

Illustrations offers many children a visual way to think through the ideas they will incorporate and to share those ideas in images as well as words. For some, visually representing the content precedes writing, and the illustrating process is an important way to order ideas that will then be put into writing. Other children use illustrations to amplify content, either literally representing information or characters and events or conveying the affective quality of their writing indirectly through covers, borders, and other decoration. Raw materials with unusual textures, shadings, or shapes and a variety of tools for applying color to images or print encourage thoughtful development of illustrations. Special papers are sometimes reserved for illustrations, and unique materials for book binding or mounting for display support the extension of expression through illustration.

Sharing and feedback provide important information to children about their own writing and the writing of others. The sharing process may highlight alternative ways of expressing ideas and events in the displayed writing of different people and provide pleasure as children read one another's work. Observations in literacy environments show that children are especially interested in their classmates' writing and attend to current child-initiated displayed print with great eagerness, although they ignore print that isn't current.

Writers feel their work is appreciated when they see somebody reading it, and sometimes peers provide written feedback. The feedback about the clarity of their writing that comes from readers' understanding and enjoyment of their work offers a powerful stimulus for further development and editing of language and style. The provisions that support sharing and feedback also support other activities throughout the day. Book racks, gallery-like appreciative display, special places to feature individual pieces of writing, and book-binding materials all encourage children to share their writing.

Responses from peers, outside of the formal feedback arranged in the instructional program, are helpful to children who wish to extend their writing. Sometimes children display sign-ons beside their work, asking for written feedback; in many environments children make it a point to speak directly to an author about the displayed work. The display facilities make sharing possible, making feedback more likely, which in turn often sends children to the process of editing.

Editing, the review and revision of writing for clearer or more effective ways of organizing and presenting ideas, is different from proofreading (checking for accuracy in conventions), although they may occur at the same time. Sometimes children do their own proofreading, without peer help, but working with somebody is important for editing. Editing is encouraged by provisions such as clearly identifiable draft paper and final copy paper and a variety of recording tools, some erasable (because they are intended for drafts that undergo many changes as they develop) and others for permanent, finished copies. Dictionaries and other conventions references are necessary, and for serious editing additional references such as a thesaurus and displayed models of good writing in descriptions, summaries, or dialogue are important. Small-group work spaces enable children to go off together to share competencies, and offer them separation from the other events in the environment while they concentrate on editing.

Extending Self-Initiated Writing

- Collaborating
- Talking out plans
- Trying out ideas in print
- Illustrating
- Sharing writing
- Receiving feedback
- Proof reading and editing

THE TEACHER'S ENVIRONMENTAL ROLE

Teachers contribute to children's spontaneous writing in several ways. They arrange space and materials to support the ongoing processes and stimulate new writing projects, model some of the processes of writing, and briefly interact with children as they work in the environment. They look for evidence of children's growth in their products and in the ways they use the environment and interact with their peers about their writing.

Stimulating and Supporting Writing

Writing is a literacy function of the environment that requires special attention to the visual qualities of arrangements for print and for provisions. The examples and models of print for use as references must be extremely clear, so children can easily perceive the forms and details of every part. Arrangements that enable children to display their own writings in a visually clear setting are essential to receiving feedback. The information sources and other provisions that stimulate the flow of ideas and stories are highlighted through display, so they have the capacity to engage children and involve them with the ideas they represent. Teachers often select unusual provisions, such as special papers for final copies or unusual book-binding materials, because of particular visual qualities that will set off a good piece of writing.

As children work in the environment, teachers have brief exchanges with them about writing. Sometimes teachers listen to children as they read a sentence or a short story aloud; they speak to a child about the feelings expressed in their writing and acknowledge children's accomplishments; sometimes teachers take a few moments to find a special book and read a passage aloud for a child who will understand the efforts and the meaning of its author.

There are moments when teachers can model aspects of the writing process while children are working. Teachers make sure children see them writing and editing newsletters and reports, and they find ways to share the final products with the children.

Looking for Evidence of Growth

Information about growth in writing is found in displayed written products, in the way the environment's resources are used, and in work with peers during the writing process.

When the environment provides containers for short-term storage of work in progress, teachers see evidence of understandings and competence in children's drafts and later in the final copies they choose to display for others to read. Their proofreading and editing abilities are shown clearly when both early drafts and final editions are read.

The depth of children's involvement in their own spontaneous writing is often revealed in the way they display their work. When children illustrate carefully and display the illustration with the writing, or when they place special objects beside the displayed writing to emphasize some central theme in the writing, teachers can easily see a child's commitment and the intense personal meaning the writing holds for its author.

Teachers observe children's competence with the writing process through glimpses of children at work in the environment. They demonstrate their use of references, the ability to collaborate with others in the writing process, and their developing competence with the processes of proofreading and editing, as well as the maturity with which they receive feedback and act upon it in the development of their writing.

Book Use

Definitions of the word "literate" include two aspects: having the ability to read and write and being acquainted with writings. The use of books is closely associated with the meaning of literacy, and research identifies relationships between experiences with books and several literacy behaviors, such as reading progress, self-initiated involvement in literature, and valuing literacy (Martin, 1979).

Books have traditionally played an important role in teachers' direct instructional work; however, children's involvement with books is not exclusively dependent on teacher-designed activities. The learning environment can be deliberately arranged to instigate and support book-related activities throughout the day, without teacher intervention.

BOOKS AND THE GROWTH OF LITERACY

It is clear that a curriculum with literacy growth as a goal demands involvement with books. Literacy includes not only the ability to read and write for a variety of purposes; it also includes valuing reading and writing enough to use those literacy behaviors as a part of daily life. Therefore, the literacy environment, with its capacity to elicit these behaviors, offers important extensions to the formal use of books in the instructional program, encouraging children to function as literate persons while steadily increasing their competency.

Reading Progress and Books

The many connections between children's experiences with books and progress in learning to read are so strong that even simple book-handling knowledge is a good predictor of children's movement toward reading, and storytelling with book language shows a child's understanding of differences between conversational and literary forms of language. Studies of children who were early readers show that a large number and variety of experiences with books precede children's learning to read. Being read to, having favorite books, and observing family members using books were among the experiences the early readers had in common (Durkin, 1966).

Research about the reading process (Goodman, 1977) suggests that familiarity with literary forms increases a reader's effectiveness in predicting what comes next in text. Experiences with literature in both home and school settings enable prereaders to become familiar with many different forms; this familiarity develops anticipation of predictable language patterns. Reading to children who can already read is important also, helping them expand their familiarity with a wide range of literary language, which in turn helps them increase the effectiveness of their predictions. Children are most successful in predicting when dealing with language they have produced themselves or with text familiar through many hearings. And it seems that the quantity of print and language richness of the texts children encounter as they try to read is related to their reading progress (Holdaway, 1984).

Several kinds of book and print-based experiences have been identified as strong, positive influences on the development of reading: children observing and emulating adults using reading to meet daily

Reading to children
builds ability to
predict language.

purposes; participating in reading aloud with others; practicing reading stories that have been read aloud to them (Holdaway, 1984). Stories often read aloud by request become familiar and safe, leading children to choose and practice these books again and again.

The Utility of Books

From the time language usage begins, children ask questions and make direct investigations into the qualities and functions of their surroundings, and this basic characteristic continues through school years. As children grow, their inquiry becomes more focused and skillful, but the hunger for information and interest in a great range of topics and questions remains (Alberty & Weber, 1979), and they are drawn to books offering pertinent information. Children need a great deal of information as they struggle to make sense of their natural and social environments, and books are an invaluable help. They function as information sources, whether encyclopedia, almanac, dictionary, textbook, novel, poetry, or some other print form. Whatever the book, the context, and the setting, the reader's viewpoint determines how useful it is. New information leads them to new questions, and a cycle develops as questions lead to books for answers that satisfy, and in turn lead to new questions and back again to other books (Georgiou, 1969).

Children see the utility of reading as they encounter interesting and satisfying information in books shared with adults and watch family members find informational books to help them carry out important projects (Taylor, 1983). Related classroom experiences reinforce these positive attitudes for children who already see books as useful, and help others learn to value books. References and other information books are treasured as much as fiction when read aloud, offering experiences that are satisfying because they provide information, support developing curiosity, and foster positive feelings about books as a source of information (Martin, 1974).

Literature Experiences

Children's literature contributes to the acquisition of reading ability, of course, but it also has its own importance. The magic, the mystery, the fact, fiction, and fancy of creative literature for and by children is a confirmation of childhood itself (Egoff, Stubbs & Ashley, 1980). Literature for children as for adults gives enjoyment, helps develop imagination, provides vicarious experience, offers insight into human behavior, and highlights aspects of experience that are universal. Children from book-loving families have "probably heard more than a thousand bedtime stories" before ever coming to school (Huck, 1976), and in those stories they have encountered feelings, ideas, and experiences that both confirm and extend their own. High book use environments provide similar experiences for children who do not receive this supportive start at home.

A FUNCTIONING LITERACY ENVIRONMENT

An environment for literacy reflects to some degree all these personal experiences known to be related to literacy development. The environment provides support for book use, helping children develop literary tastes and interests, establish habits of using books in daily activities, and practice silent and oral reading skills.

Classroom books that connect to children's lives and offer useful information for their activities help them value reading for its utility. Books chosen for literary qualities of language and form demonstrate the pleasure that books bring when they help children reach beyond the boundaries of their immediate world and extend the limits of all their experiences.

A SUCCESS STORY

As recess ended, Verna Begay walked back toward her classroom, wondering if she had been too hasty when she said, "All my children read books! I know they do." Some of the teachers in the lounge had firmly asserted that there are *some* children in *every* room who do not use books, and they meant those poor or reluctant readers who don't seem to find much satisfaction in print as well as the confused or hostile ones. Verna was sure that all her children used books in their classroom, but she realized that she wouldn't be satisfied until she had checked the children's use of the books in the room to see whether she was right. As she entered the room, where the children were already returning to their work, her eye fell on the special book display by the door. She had placed the new copy of the *Secret Garden* (Burnett, 1962) on a chalk ledge with a message saying, "I first read this book when I was your age. I thought you might want to see this new edition." She had noticed several children reading the note and handling the book and later found a reply from Ramona: "Do you still have your old copy? Could we see it?" It took a few days to find the box where it was stored away, and by the time she brought it in, Andrea had added another edition and taped a note by it saying: "This was my grandmother's book." Now seven different copies were displayed, and several of the girls had started drawing pictures to go with each edition date.

Rafael needed another approach to books. When he first came several months ago, he was an apparent nonreader both in English and in his mother tongue, Spanish. All efforts to get him to try to read met with failure, until the day when a parent brought a Polaroid camera to the classroom. The parents supplied everyone with a photograph of them working or exhibiting some project. After school that day Mrs. Begay arranged some tape, some staplers, and special book-cover paper with some of the snapshots in a larger work space. The next morning several of the children started making books, using their pictures to illustrate the work they wrote about. When she saw Rafael staring at his picture while sitting at a table surrounded by book-making materials, she mentioned that if he would like to say something about his picture she would write it for him. Shyly, after several starts and hesitations, Rafael dictated: "I am Rafael. I am in the fifth grade. Mrs. Begay is my teacher. This is my book." With those words and that one picture, Rafael started using the materials in front of him. When Mrs. Begay gave him a snapshot of her, he asked her to add to his story. Rafael read and reread his book.

One morning she found him at a table where several books were displayed, looking at some of the personal books made by the other children. When no one else was around, she offered to help him read one of the books he picked out. Over the next few days Rafael read from one personal book, then another, and from then on began to handle, then later study, other types of displayed books.

Mrs. Begay noticed Leon next, with his paper, pencils, and several reference books, so involved with his reading that he hadn't heard her come into the room. He was described by previous teachers as a poor, reluctant, and hostile reader, but before she had a chance to check these things for herself, she had found him in front of a display of pottery shards and some other artifacts, looking furiously from the realia to the accompanying books. Before the morning was over, he had used the nearby recording tools to compare the artifacts in the class collection and those pictured in the books and had made a list of other references he wanted to get from the library. Leon was intensely interested in reading accurate information, in references, magazines, or instructional materials, but his mother and earlier teachers had been disappointed when he wasn't interested in fiction or the basal reader stories that interested them. Leon was one of the best readers and most productive writers in the room, but it was true: He didn't read fiction and other dramatic forms.

Marie, who would hardly read anything but fiction, was in a quiet and private spot with her nose in a book. So far the only extension Mrs. Begay had managed to elicit was the informational reading Marie needed to complete classroom projects. She would read carefully the instructions for care of the animals, or the animal cages, and keep cumulative records on the number and kinds of books checked from the library, with a tally of the class preferences. Maybe there was some way Leon and Marie could extend each other's interests and experiences.

As the day passed Mrs. Begay recalled each child who she already knew used the environment's informational and recreational books extensively. She watched carefully for those about whom she wasn't so certain. Melissa, now reading a story to entertain a group of children finishing some artwork, had explained to the teacher one day that she and her brothers and sisters often picked a "weekly reader" at home to read stories to the others as they did their chores.

Joseph was reading bike safety information to a group that had helped Mrs. Begay establish a display of manuals for vehicle care and safety. Peter claimed he knew all the bike information, so he was studying a driver's manual.

One by one, the teacher identified the reading habits of all the children. She had examples of everyone choosing to use books. Some used books much more than others; some became involved with a much wider spectrum of literacy forms than others. But it was there. There were books for every purpose, for every interest, somewhere in the learning environment; and the children all used books, as well as other print information, in the room.

SUPPORTING BOOK EXPERIENCES

Carefully provisioned environments maintain and extend book experiences beyond those directly supervised by the teacher. Listening to teachers read books is extended through experiences such as reading aloud (Holdaway, 1979), revisiting familiar read-aloud books, hearing new stories read aloud, and reading stories to classmates. Environmental arrangements can encourage and support these experiences.

The environment itself can promote awareness of books, create possibilities for children to listen to favorite stories again and again, suggest rereading of books already heard, encourage responses to literature, and highlight the utility of informational books. A variety of forms and types of books expands the interests that can be supported and the range of literacy behaviors elicited. The likelihood that children will initiate their own book experiences is increased by environmental arrangements presenting books related to every activity and every material in every area. Such arrangements are instrumental in helping children acquire a lifelong recognition of the value of book reading.

Hearing Books

Being read to can be enjoyable at all ages and is important for literacy growth throughout elementary school. Most teachers read books to groups of children; additional opportunities to hear teachers read books aloud are created by provisioning work spaces with recorded readings and accompanying books.

Many children choose to listen to their teachers reading fiction, and they enjoy the familiarity and predictability of known stories. However, as they grow older, children often prefer to listen to informational books, so teachers record both stories and nonfiction related to current curriculum content and to the interests of their children. The tapes enable children to listen to the same books read aloud again and again, and many children who have heard a familiar story on tape numerous times will request the book again when teachers are reading directly to them.

Young children enjoy hearing tapes of their teacher reading aloud some of their own group- or individually-dictated stories. Arrangements combining labeled tape cassettes with a displayed copy of the recorded book or story help children identify the story they wish to hear and also give them an opportunity to look at the print of the story while listening.

Children listen to their teacher read stories on tape.

Peer reading is another way to hear books read aloud. Teachers may prepare sign-on charts asking children if they want to read aloud to classmates, perhaps identifying the time and the book; some individuals who wish to read aloud post invitations, asking listeners to sign. Special collections help younger readers select books they can read aloud well; older children may read aloud because they want to share part of a book they have enjoyed, so they often select from a wider base of literature. Peer reading is supported by spatial organization that creates a variety of small-group areas through furniture placement defining spaces and offering separation between areas.

Reading Along

Cassette tapes of teachers reading familiar books are very popular. Work spaces for individuals or very small groups, provisioned with a tape player and a few tapes accompanied by the book itself, make it possible for a person to read the story along with the teacher. With earphones and multiple copies of a book, three or four children can enjoy the reading along together. While they are wearing earphones, children aren't always aware how loud their voices are, so it's useful to have some sound shelter in an area with earphones. Fabric on the back of a cabinet, pillows rather than chairs, or other arrangements creating softness absorb some of the sound in an area.

A small group of children can read along with one another in a work space displaying some Big Books they have enjoyed earlier with the teacher, or they can read along using duplicate copies of familiar books. The invitation to read along is arranged through the careful display of two or three copies of a book in an organizer showing the covers clearly, within a space where a few children can be together.

Revisiting Read-aloud Books

Books that have been first heard in the social setting of a group listening to the teacher read aloud become very inviting and important to children. Opportunities to return to those books extend the enjoyment of the experience and support children's literacy growth. Reading along, becoming involved in handling the book, looking through its illustrations, or working with the text are satisfying and important activities.

Some read-aloud books are placed in the environment for children's use only after they have been presented by the teacher, so clear display that reminds children about the books' availability prompts revisiting. These books are often placed in a special exhibit for a few days after they have been read aloud, and children are reminded of their interest in particular volumes as they see the display; after a few days the books are relocated in various places around the environment. Some read-aloud books, associated with particular interests, are displayed in areas holding related materials. For instance, a storybook about a child exploring magnets is displayed beside a tray holding several magnets and a small collection of materials to test the magnet; the invitation to revisit the book comes from both the book and the materials. A few small work spaces, where children can have privacy as they revisit or reread books, enables some children to become deeply involved in their reading.

Reading for Different Purposes

Children's purposes for reading books grow out of activities stimulated by the environment's provisions, which are deliberately arranged to lead children to books. Books are placed in areas with raw materials, tools, nonprint information sources; sometimes the provisions are moved to new locations to highlight particular books.

Children search through reference books to find specific information when materials that capture their interest are arranged close to the

Books are placed with raw materials and tools.

references, and they select informational books to gather a broader base of information. They read other informational books to find out how to construct, cook, or carry out experiments that are suggested by arrangements of materials and tools. Children read current magazines to verify opinions and to find out more about community concerns and events connected with written comments or photographs of the community. They read stories set in other places and times to gain insights into life in various settings, called to their attention through displayed illustrations or nearby filmstrips available for their independent use. They use raw materials and tools organized for their access to make puppets or a stage, then read plays for ideas for their performances. They read catalogues to gather price lists and compare the attributes of different models of equipment the class is raising money for, when the catalogues are near a sign-on chart asking for recommendations. Such reading experiences in a variety of contexts and with a range of purposes, stimulated by environmental arrangements, help children value reading for its pleasures and utility as they extend and reinforce the teacher's planned program for books.

EXPLORING BOOKS

It's easy to see, looking around a literacy environment, that books are important to teachers and children, because they are everywhere. Arrangements for browsing, sharing, and special displays heighten awareness of all the books, so classroom collections seem much larger than those seen in rooms without such emphasis. However, arrangements that promote children's self-initiated book experiences can fill a room with books that could be stored, library style, in a single bookcase in the corner of a classroom, where many would remain unused; it is the arrangements, rather than just quantity, that encourages children to explore and share books.

Browsing

Arrangements that gather a group of books together and display them so the covers are visible urge children to linger and handle the books, look through the illustrations or chapter headings, and turn the pages. Several browsing arrangements in an environment make it possible for the collections to change fairly often and to feature different book qualities or contents from time to time. A browsing collection is sometimes a random selection of books that haven't been chosen by children for a while, or it may be a collection by an author, informational and fictional books about a particular historical period, or a collection connected to some seasonal community event such as holidays, fiestas, fairs, or other celebrations.

A piece of molding across the back of a cabinet that defines a pathway can hold a browsing collection of seven or eight volumes, while floor space just under the chalkboard is sometimes used to stand books for another collection. Browsing collections beckon from areas where children gather for group sessions, near pathways wide enough for some to browse and others to pass, beneath a central message board, in a corner that seems too small to provision for activity, on the window sill, on a shelf above low coat hooks but still within reach, and many other locations.

Sometimes there are featured collections for browsing, usually arranged in some prominent place by children and teachers, which may invite others to add to the collection. They may be books from home, seasonal books found in the library, or books that have a common feature someone has found intriguing.

Sharing

Like other literacy activities, children's self-initiated experiences with books are more often social than private; sometimes two children enjoy looking at the same book, and even when a good book is read alone, a person wants to talk about it with somebody else who has also read it. Social settings that accommodate book sharing often contain browsing collections and sometimes display duplicate copies of very popular books related to other provisions in the area.

Raw materials, display facilities, and tools, displayed in each area along with its books, encourage a variety of responses. Children may draw a scene or episode from a book that has been vivid to them as they read, write, and display quotations. Sometimes they comment on a book they are sure others would enjoy and display the comments with a publisher's or child-made book jacket, or they may arrange comments with the book in a display that highlights it. Some children make and display their own books, extending plots or information they have read or creating stories on familiar themes.

Children who have found books a satisfying source of information for their study often share that information. They read passages to one another, comparing information; they pool the information gathered by several people from several references; and they make summaries and compilations. The inclination to share information from books is spurred by provisions arranged for that purpose in each area where children work.

BOOKS FOR THE ENVIRONMENT

Book selection for the learning environment is determined by the functions of the environment in providing support for children's learning activities and in fostering general literacy growth. There are many excellent criteria for specific book selection presented in the context of the study of children's literature, and it is important to apply those criteria to the teacher's decision making about the literature program. The discussion here focuses only on the learning environment and its capacity to foster spontaneous involvement with the use of books in self-initiated learning activities.

Many kinds of books are required to support the interests and activities of a group of involved learners. Variation in the kinds available for children's use influences the purposes for which books are used and the extent to which children with different reading preferences become involved.

Different Kinds of Books

Almost every classroom is provisioned with some basic textbooks; these tend to be multiple-copy sets, intended for use in instructional sessions. Textbooks are also very useful when arranged for children's self-initiated involvement with books, when single copies of various texts are present, representing several grade-level designations. Borrowing one copy of each subject-matter text from each grade level in the school ensures a collection of very useful information sources, providing considerable variation in details and difficulty and meeting the interests and competence of a larger number of individuals. Reference books are a bit like single-copy texts. One copy of many different titles frequently attracts much more interest, and certainly provides more information, than many copies of the same title.

Both fiction and nonfiction trade books bring to the literacy environment something for every interest and appetite. Children's activities, their questions, and their suggestions are useful guides to the selection of trade books. Teachers also select on the basis of the curriculum and their knowledge of specific children and their growth.

Children's fiction enables readers to make new discoveries, consult illustrations, enjoy new authors and styles, and read aloud, listen, or read along with others. Traditional stories encourage children to revisit favorites met when they were younger. Informational books may support the planned curriculum, provide useful or interesting material for a given learner's needs, or reflect and support other materials and activities within the learning environment.

Many specialized informational books, not designed for specific use as classroom information sources, are important provisions. Music books, arranged near records and tapes of songs or beside musical instruments, capture the interests of many children, who may sing along with records or find familiar songs in the books to sing with some friends. Cookbooks, appliance manuals, self-help guides, telephone directories, catalogues, government publications, travel books, and magazines are other examples of the different kinds of books that stimulate and support children's spontaneous involvement when they are connected to the activities and interests of the group.

Books for the Literacy Environment

- Magazines
- Informational trade books
- Music books
- Picture books
- Biographies
- Pamphlets
- Self-help books
- Travel books
- Appliance manuals
- Cook books
- Reference books
- Textbooks
- Government publications
- Directories
- Fiction trade books
- Catalogues

Nothing replaces the uniqueness of personal, handmade books. These books—made by the teacher, other adults, individual children, or a whole group or class, sometimes highly professional in artwork, binding, and content, and sometimes presenting the first words of beginning writers on corner-stapled scrap paper—have a relevance and identity to be treasured. Young children may become involved for the first time by rereading dictated stories where they are the heroes; more sophisticated readers and writers collect personal and local history, keep records, and present work in many creative forms. These personal books tend to create interest because they are made by or for a friend or provide stories and information about familiar events or people.

Big Books, oversized versions of favorite stories for young children, are often made by parents or teachers so a group can see, touch, and read the same book together. Other teacher-made books include anthologies of favorite poetry, collections of children's illustrated or dictated stories, or perhaps chronological collections of group experiences or some project records. Work spaces provisioned for writing, illustrating, and book binding support children in writing and crafting handmade books, and ample space for book display makes it possible for these books to take their place alongside other kinds of publications.

Special Considerations

The content of books supporting children's interest and activities involve a wide range of topics and themes emerging from diverse sources, such as extensions of the formal curriculum, individual curiosity, and the need of growing children, to reflect on those personal experiences that are reflected in literature about the lives of others.

A wide range of difficulty levels makes any collection more useful. Most teachers understand that any group of children includes readers and writers of widely varying proficiency; this alone is sufficient reason for provisioning with variety in difficulty level. Children's growth in literacy demands materials that provide ease and comfort in self-initiated reading and materials to stretch and stimulate interests and competencies (Olson, 1952, Spring).

The quantity of books for a classroom collection always seems to be a problem. Few teachers think there are enough in the environment, but there is no formula to determine what quantity is necessary to make the use of books an integral part of life in the literacy environment. It seems clear that the usefulness of any collection for children's literacy activities can be extended when the books are well distributed and clearly displayed so that they receive maximum use, that variety in the kinds and content of the books is more important than quantity alone, and that quantity over time may be just as useful as quantity at any given time.

Adding to Book Collections

A functioning literacy environment requires much more extensive provisioning than the basic supplies, books, and equipment ordinarily provided for elementary classrooms. This means that teachers provision in a very active way, extending the materials that are available, joining with other teachers in community contacts, planning for and rotating materials among classrooms, trading, borrowing, and scrounging. Provisioning, which includes searching, obtaining, and sharing materials for the classroom, has been discussed extensively elsewhere (Loughlin & Suina, 1982), so the brief discussion here considers only some general sources for additional books.

Classroom and school libraries are a primary available resource; they provide a basic core of books to arrange and display around the environment and supplement those from other libraries. City or county libraries lend collections of children's books and are especially appropriate places for a teacher to appeal to for help with a special, single topic. In some parts of the country, state libraries help supply needed books, particularly in areas where school, city, or county sources are limited.

Many teachers use garage sales and flea markets to provide cheap, occasionally rare, and often very welcome additions. Children and their families help teachers nose out special sales, make hauls from family attics or other discards, and even make temporary loans of personal books for special purposes. When teachers are trying to meet similar book needs, temporary exchanges and other kinds of sharing are helpful. When teachers make their own classroom library selections, cooperative planning with sharing as a goal can make a school's budget go further. Children's book fairs and used-book sales are popular fund raisers in many communities; they call attention to the books and the need to expand the available selections and sometimes provide additions to classroom collections at little or no cost.

BOOK DISPLAY

Some of the best examples of effective book display are found in bookstores and other retail settings where magazines and paperbacks are marketed. Materials are clearly displayed in racks that present them face out, with both print and pictures serving as invitations. The face of the cover or jacket gives enticing information, while illustrations capture interest and perhaps encourage potential buyers to leaf through a volume. Special books, like best-sellers or new releases, are often displayed alone or in special groups, combined with other information designed to increase interest or curiosity, in case the colorful covers aren't sufficient. Sellers' strategies are effective in the learning environment also, when the beautiful and informative covers and book jackets of children's books encourage interest and use, which in turn lead to continuous book involvement.

Displaying books is more demanding than displaying other forms of print, because the significant information identifying a book is located on the front surface, as it is on the paper that carries displayed print, yet the books are three-dimensional objects and aren't easily tacked on bulletin boards or taped to a vertical surface. So teachers use classroom book-display furniture, such as bookcases or book racks and empty desks tops, to display some books with the covers visible, and they improvise ways to display the rest. They make book easels out of corrugated cardboard, book racks from pegboard and wood; they persuade book shops and newsstands and drugstores to donate book racks they no longer use; and they involve children and parents in construction of others.

Books in the literacy environment are displayed in racks, on ledges and sills, along edges, and on the tops of furniture. They are hung with string and Velcro strips, or are clipped to wire, pegboards, trellises, and clotheslines. Books stand upright in small racks on the sides of cabinets, on the top of coatracks and teachers' desks, in hanging wire baskets, on molding strips along the back of large cabinets, on pegboard brackets, on windowsills and chalk ledges, on the floor along the edges of areas, on racks attached to closet doors, and in any other places where books can rest upright, with covers clearly displayed.

Book display is often improvised.

Books are displayed in plastic pockets, in fabric book-display bags, and in cardboard pocket charts.

Single books are featured by arrangements on turntables, small easels, and lecterns, or by arrangements that include interesting objects that hint at the book's content. They are placed on temporary stands covered with fabric, arranged in front of a textured or beautifully colored backdrop, or set out with accompanying materials on a surface that holds nothing else.

THE TEACHER'S ENVIRONMENTAL ROLE

Behind the scenes, teachers reorganize the environment to encourage and sustain productive involvement with books, and they read the environment to learn more about children's growth, reflecting on their exchanges with and glimpses of children as they use and contribute to the environment's stimulus for book use. In many brief moments of interaction, as children use the environment, teachers suggest books, share pleasure over a particular illustration, listen to a special passage, exchange comments about accuracy of information, talk about authors; these exchanges help to sustain children's self-initiated involvement with books. Teachers model the use of books by reading to themselves and others, looking up information in reference books, talking about a book sent to them by another person, or looking through new books to make book order selections.

Teachers also introduce books by arranging special displays, such as collections organized around seasons, authors, genres, illustrators, or topics and through special displays of single volumes. They maintain children's interest by moving books from one place to another, removing some books for a short while, and adding others. These decisions are based on the patterns of book use, changing interests and events, and observations of children's responses to books.

EVIDENCE OF GROWTH

Brief observations and glimpses of children using books in self-initiated activities offer teachers some important information about growth in literacy. Teachers note who browses, who searches for particular content, and who is not yet involved with the books. They notice children struggling to read self-chosen books that stretch their competence, because reading that particular book is important to

Teachers arrange
special displays.

them. They notice who asks others to read to them and who reads to others.

Records of book check-outs, organized as sign-on charts or in other ways, offer information about children's reading preferences and the extent of their book use. Displayed products, created in response to book experiences, indicate the ways in which children have understood the writers, as well as showing something of children's abilities to summarize or represent ideas in writing or illustration.

10

Analyzing the Environment

The functioning literacy environment is an example of the fourth environmental task, arranging for special purposes. The basic environmental framework is established by teachers through the tasks of spatial organization, provisioning, and materials arrangement; these influence children's literacy behavior in the same way they influence other behaviors. Consequently, any environment for literacy must first be a functioning *learning* environment; no amount of literacy can create a functioning literacy environment unless that environment already effectively supports children's learning activities.

Analysis of literacy begins with the analysis of the whole environment: its space, its provisioning framework, and its materials arrangement. That process is presented fully elsewhere (Loughlin & Suina, 1982); the discussion here focuses on the analysis of literacy, with the assumption that such an analysis is preceded by a review of the total environment.

When a teacher organizes the environment for the special purpose of supporting spontaneous uses of literacy behaviors, it is essential to know whether the environmental arrangements are likely to promote those behaviors; analyzing the environment through a survey of literacy materials can show whether children will encounter extensive encouragement for literacy activity and whether suggestions for literacy exist throughout the environment or only in certain areas. A careful survey also makes it possible to predict the uses of literacy activity most likely to occur, prompted by the particular kinds of literacy stimuli children encounter during the day.

The environment's potential ability to instigate and support children's spontaneous literacy activity can be analyzed by examining the literacy stimuli displayed throughout the environment, noting where they are located and what kinds they are. The Survey of Displayed Literacy Stimuli (shown in full in Appendix A) is a tool designed for that analysis.

THE SURVEY OF DISPLAYED LITERACY

The Survey of Displayed Literacy Stimuli (Loughlin & Cole, 1986) identifies particular materials and certain arrangements of materials seen in classrooms where children are extremely active in literacy. Although there are many other materials that adults associate with literacy, the survey includes only items children have responded to by incorporating literacy into their activities.

The survey was developed as a tool to describe a literacy environment in terms of its stimulus level and to compare one literacy environment with another, or one part of a single environment with another part (Cole & Loughlin, 1984). The original categories of literacy stimuli were constructed on the basis of a conceptualization of a literacy environment (Loughlin, 1982) and placed in a checklist designed to help teachers assess their own environments (Sheehan & Cole, 1983). The checklist was applied to the analysis of a large number of classrooms in which teachers consciously developed the environment to promote the use of literacy; then information from observations of children spontaneously using displayed literacy materials were compared to the lists. Over several years in which the survey was studied and developed through continuous use, categories were added, removed, combined, and defined on the basis of their ability to include displayed literacy materials that engaged children's interest and influenced their uses of literacy in the observed classrooms.

The survey now has two major applications. It has become an extremely useful tool for teacher development in relation to the literacy environment (Ivener, 1983) when used for individual self-study or in ongoing workshops and study groups, and it is a useful descriptive tool for research because it can distinguish between high- and low-stimulus–level classrooms. The descriptions of literacy arrangements presented in the preceding chapters are taken from the high-stimulus–level classrooms observed during the development of the survey and during later research in which the survey was used.

THE DISPLAYED LITERACY STIMULI

The Survey of Displayed Literacy Stimuli includes sixteen categories of arrangements and materials for literacy, which serve as a checklist in the examination of a single area of a classroom. An environment is surveyed, area by area, for instances of each category of literacy stimulus; these are either counted or noted as present in the area, then recorded.

Counted Categories

Some categories of displayed literacy stimuli are counted as each area is surveyed. The information is used to describe the level and pattern of the environment's literacy support. The counted categories, with definitions, follow.

Current child-generated messages, labels, or stories must be less than five days old. These may be written or dictated. Age is determined by dated material or by asking. Groups of completed assignments displayed together are excluded from this category. Items counted here may also be counted in another category.

Messages about the current day include schedules, assignments, notices, groupings, news, and announcements needed to work through the day. These are clearly related to events on the day of the survey.

Displayed directions for activities are displayed task cards or charts that give directions for activities or procedures that children can carry out independently. Labels that explain how to operate equipment or care for material are excluded.

Sign-on charts or sheets are any teacher- or child-prepared sheet, clearly displayed, that calls for children to record information in print or symbol or to sign names.

Different kinds of books mean a count of the kinds of books available for children's access, displayed so they are clearly visible (i.e., trade, reference, child-made, magazines, etc.). The number of volumes is *not* counted.

Different kinds of recording tools refer to the number of different kinds of tools for children's use in recording events, ideas, information (i.e., pencils, crayons, chalk, tape recorders, etc.). Duplicates in an area are *not* counted.

Different kinds of recording materials refer to the number of different kinds of materials for children to record upon (i.e., audiotape, stationery, chart paper, chalkboard, drawing paper, etc.). Duplicates in an area are *not* counted.

Different references mean lists, pictures, charts, or other information sources children may use as references to help with ongoing activities. A set of references (i.e., an encyclopedia) stored together is counted as one reference. Single volumes placed in different locations are counted. Duplicates in an area are *not* counted.

Print or writing segments related to nearby materials, objects, or pictures are placed close to pictures or other materials, with the contents of the print or writing clearly related to those materials in some way. Labels are excluded. Children's illustrated stories are excluded, unless they are related to other nearby materials.

Books related to nearby materials, objects, or pictures are books located in combination with other materials, objects, or pictures and whose contents are clearly related to those materials in some way.

Community culture/language books or print segments are books and print segments written in children's home language, or reflecting home culture, in a fairly homogeneous linguistic/cultural community not ordinarily represented in educational materials.

Noted Categories

Several categories in the survey are not counted, but their presence or absence is noted in each area. These displayed literacy stimuli combine with other materials in any area to convey an encouragement for literacy. The presence of these materials in all areas contributes significantly to the uses of literacy across the environment. The categories and their definitions follow.

Presence of empty display space refers to empty space in the area that is clearly available for children to display their own work. This is not always labeled and can be determined by indications that materials have been displayed there, by something already displayed but not using all the space, or by asking.

Presence of display tools refers to visibly displayed tacks, tape, label blanks, and/or other tools children can use to display materials.

Presence of clearly legible handwritten or machine-printed segments describes print and child or teacher writing, displayed on unpatterned background with empty space surrounding the segment. Print or writing is large enough to be seen by children in the area.

Presence of books with cover or page displayed refers to books in the area with the covers clearly visible, displayed, or with a particular page clearly visible.

Presence of functional labels refers to working labels on holders, cabinets, or equipment that give information about contents, use, or procedures for use.

USING THE SURVEY

Every classroom houses materials associated with literacy that do not fulfill the functions of displayed literacy stimuli. There is some basic information about literacy materials that makes it easier to use the survey effectively; the general procedures, and the reasons for them, are discussed below. Specific directions are shown on the cover page of the survey, which is shown as Exhibit 1 in Appendix A.

Patterns of Distribution

A person surveying an environment first examines spatial organization, draws a sketch map of the room, then marks the boundaries of several areas within it. In some classrooms, where space isn't divided, the sketch map is just divided into five or six sections. In most classrooms furniture is used to divide different activity areas, so the boundaries of those areas are used. It is important to include *all* the environment's space as boundaries are drawn, so spaces near an entry way or the center of the room are also shown. The names of the areas are written on the sketch map and the record form; then the environment is surveyed one area at a time, to reveal the patterns of distribution, as well as the quantity of displayed literacy stimuli.

The survey is used area by area because it is not enough to know which stimuli are in the environment, or even how many. Literacy stimuli are effective only when children see them, so their placement influences children's behaviors as strongly as does their category; it's important to know *where* the stimuli are located. Many children remain in one or two locations all day, from preference or because they are assigned there. The pattern of displayed literacy stimuli shows both the intensity and the kinds of stimuli a child encounters in those areas, and the information helps teachers understand and predict each child's involvement in literacy.

Categories as a Checklist

To survey one area, a person enters the area and from *children's eye level* looks around the environment to see it as children do. Then, with recording sheet and definitions (Appendix A, Exhibits 2 and 3) in hand, the surveyor reads one category definition and looks carefully around the area for materials or arrangements that match that definition and are fully visible. The number or the presence of items is recorded. Each area is examined for one category at a time until information about all categories has been recorded.

It is important to remember that the survey is a checklist; it does not attempt to categorize everything in an environment. There are literacy materials in many areas that do not fit into any of the categories; they do not function as literacy stimuli. The surveyor begins by looking at a category, then searching the environment for items that fit the category. It isn't appropriate to look first at materials and then struggle to place them on the checklist, because the materials may not fit any category.

Materials have been excluded from the survey if, after numerous observations in many settings, children were not seen using them in self-initiated activity. This means that such materials did not stimulate their own use. A displayed literacy stimulus is a stimulus for activity. To function as a stimulus, the material must be clearly seen. Where there is a stimulus, there must also be the means to respond to that stimulus, so children can engage in literacy activity. Materials were not included in the survey if they were not displayed. It was clear children did not use materials stored away even though they seemed potentially available for classroom use. Those above eye level were used only when other stimuli prompted their use. Materials displayed out of reach or materials with no arrangement enabling children to carry out suggested literacy actions made no contribution.

Counted and Noted Categories

Materials for eleven categories in the survey are counted: in every area the number of visible materials for each category is recorded. The information shows comparisons among areas and is also used to compare one environment to another. Observations show that materials in these categories offer strong suggestions for the use of literacy; children notice and use them throughout the day. Some of these literacy materials are traditionally associated with one activity area rather than others; however, children respond to them in a variety of settings. Data from the counted categories offer a description of the relative emphasis on different kinds of literacy activity and where in the environment that emphasis is located.

For five categories the presence of materials in the area is noted, rather than counted. When materials from these categories are present, the use of other literacy materials in the area seems to increase. They are important everywhere, and their presence is more important than their quantity. Data from all the areas provides a description of the distribution of literacy support in the environment.

There are practical reasons for recording the noted categories in this way, too. For instance, invitations to use space for display in an area are easy to identify, but the number of things that could be displayed is not. The number of books with covers clearly visible can vary from moment to moment when children are actively involved with books; counting those still displayed produces different data at different times of day.

Special Considerations

Several questions come up when the survey is used for the first time, and a review of procedures and definitions can resolve most of them. However, some questions demand special consideration.

"Which category?" is asked for several reasons. Often, it indicates that the surveyor is picking out materials in the environment and trying to find a category to fit, rather than starting with the categories and counting examples. The question may also mean the category definitions haven't been clarified before the counting begins. Seasoned survey users report it is easy to drift from specific definitions for categories, so they find it important to refer to them each time a new area is surveyed.

A third reason for the question about which category is that the function of some literacy material isn't made explicit by its appearance, although it may be quite clear to the teacher and children in the environment. In addition, there are some categories with somewhat similar definitions. For example, when looking for displayed directions for activities, should one count the posted print beside the tape recorder that says, "If you wish to record, *first* push the red button, *then* push the button marked PLAY," or is that a functional label?

Reviewing the definitions may help solve this problem. If not, then the surveyor makes a judgment and counts the item in just one category. The single item is part of a larger picture of the environment, and the literacy stimulus level described for this environment is less likely to be changed by a potentially inaccurate judgment than it would be if the item were not recorded.

An item already recorded in one category will not be recorded in another, with one exception. Every child-written or dictated item is recorded as child generated. However, if a child has written a sign-on, or a set of directions, for example, the item will also be counted in the appropriate category.

Identifying functional labels in an area demands more investigation than other categories. It's necessary to look into labeled holders, to be sure that the label and the materials match. For many understandable reasons, nonfunctional labels can appear in almost any classroom, and it is important to verify that labels are really functional.

"Where does the total belong?" is frequently asked, because the survey record sheet has no space designated for a grand total of literacy stimuli. Subtotals of data in rows and columns on the survey sheet provide two sets of information: totals by category and totals by area. There is no grand total, because that figure does not help to describe the patterns of literacy stimulus in the environment; no optimum number of literacy stimuli has been established.

INTERPRETING THE SURVEY INFORMATION

Data from the survey can be examined by groups of categories to identify particular strengths of the literacy environment. Some groups identify contexts for the use of literacy; others focus on qualities that foster extensive involvement within all of those contexts. Materials from any category may be included as part of more than one group, since no category is necessarily tied to a single context for literacy. In the classrooms where the survey was developed, children showed individual differences in regard to the contexts that were most likely to prompt literacy activity and in the way they interpreted the suggestions of the literacy stimuli. There were also characteristics of stimuli that heightened the probability of literacy activity for everybody.

A survey summary sheet (Appendix A, Exhibit 4) can be used to review the data from the survey for groups of categories. The summary sheet also shows other patterns that are useful for analysis and planning.

Child-Generated Stimuli

Information from one category, *current child-generated messages, labels, or stories,* reveals the extent to which children generate literacy stimuli for one another. Children in literacy environments are extremely interested in displayed print that has been produced by friends and classmates, provided it is current. They spend more time with new child-generated print than with most teacher-generated print. They do not respond to the content of teacher-assigned writing products as they respond to child-generated print.

The number of displayed and current child-generated print segments is the single category of stimulus that is consistently different in high- and low-stimulus–level environments. The child-written or child-dictated print segments are a good indication of the extent to which the environment instigates child-initiated literacy behavior. They show the effects of the environment and at the same time are part of the environment's encouragement for literacy activity.

The child-generated materials are an important part of the spiral relationship between literacy stimuli and children's literacy behaviors. Since one child's current literacy product often becomes a stimulus for another child's literacy activity, the environment's literacy increases as children continue to display their writing. Current print indicates a pattern of short-term display for children's products; if quantity is high, this indicates considerable ongoing literacy activity.

The child-generated category of stimuli does not stand alone, so more information about the environment is needed to determine literacy level. However, the amount of displayed print that children generate, through writing or dictation, is a good barometer of the literacy climate and an important key to the functioning of the literacy environment.

Functional-Use Stimuli

Five categories are associated with children's functional uses of print. The survey information for those stimuli as a group shows how much and where the environment provides necessary information in print. The distribution patterns for these literacy stimuli are important; if such information is found in only one location, children are reminded to use the functional print only when in that area, or when the stimulus to do so comes from some source other than the print.

Categories included in the group are *messages about the current day*; *different references*; *displayed directions for activities*; *sign-on charts or sheets*; and *presence of functional labels*. Current-day messages display information everybody needs to function in the setting; references enable individuals to find information needed for learning activities; displayed directions help individuals or small groups carry out complex activities; and functional labels are read to find specific materials, or to operate apparatus of some kind. Sign-ons are included in this group because their most common use is functional. They are often posted by teachers or children to deal with problems and needs arising from life in the classroom.

The functional-use stimuli make a good beginning for the literacy environment. They are easy to establish and influence children's uses of literacy quite rapidly, so it is very rewarding for teachers to display them. However, it isn't quite as easy for teachers alone to maintain *current* functional print; it's not surprising that environments high in current functional-use stimuli are often high in child-generated print.

Survey information from this group shows the extent to which a demand for literacy exists in the environment. In settings high in functional-use stimuli, children consult the written information frequently and manage the day with considerable independence.

The Variety Categories

Survey information about the four variety categories of literacy stimulus show how the environment meets a wide range of individual differences. The specific literacy stimuli included in this group includes *different kinds of books*; *different kinds of recording tools*; *different kinds of recording materials*; and *different references*. In each case, it is not the number of items present, but the number of different kinds of provisions that are counted.

Every group of children presents a range of individual differences in interests, approaches to learning, reading level, and skills competence. The variety of stimuli identifies provisioning patterns that can meet some of those differences: incorporating content varied enough to capture interests, providing information in several forms to meet needs of readers and prereaders, and enabling children to retrieve and record information within their own preferred styles.

A description of the variety of provisions is also a description of the range of literacy behaviors that children use, since different materials elicit different behaviors. Book variety calls upon applications of different competencies to gain access to the information they offer and also helps expand children's views of reading. Variety in recording tools and materials encourages different forms of symbolic representation, while eliciting varied writing skills, supporting different purposes for writing, and encouraging individual literacy products. Variation in references, as defined in the survey, indicates the breadth of the actual information pool available to support diverse areas of inquiry and fosters the practice of skills in different contexts. Children are more active in uses of literacy when they have access to a variety of ways to write, illustrate, or display and when different content is available for reading and information searches than when the range of possibilities is narrow.

Content

The categories that affect the content of literacy include *print or writing segments related to nearby materials, objects or pictures*; *books related to nearby materials, objects, or pictures*; and *community cul-*

ture/language books or print segments. Survey data from these categories describe the extent to which there are interesting things to read and write about in the environment.

The first two categories describe print and books displayed with related nonprint information sources. Such arrangements supply the substance for children's literacy activities as they connect print with high-interest materials. They influence the content of children's self-initiated writing and shape the focus of self-initiated inquiry.

The third category is a powerful influence on attitudes of many children as they approach literacy materials; it is a strong contributor to holding power for children whose home life is markedly different from the school's. However, this form of encouragement is often overlooked as a way of engaging children in literacy, and where community culture and language does appear, the level is usually extremely low. In the few places where such materials exist as a functioning and ongoing part of the literacy stimulus of the environment, children return to the books and current print again and again.

Communication

Data from the communication group of displayed literacy stimuli show the intensity of support for written communication within the classroom group and the places where children will meet that emphasis. Categories in this group include *current child-generated messages, labels, or stories; presence of empty display space; presence of display tools;* and *presence of clearly legible displayed handwritten or machine print segments.*

The directness and personal nature of written communication in a continuing group setting is a strong impetus for literacy. Children take pleasure in finding messages directed to them, and they learn quickly that one way to receive a message is to send one. Personal communication is fostered by shared messages, posted and visible to others. The displayed communications become literacy stimuli, as they offer models and suggestions for written communication and increase the interesting print children encounter in the environment.

When children are actively communicating with one another in writing, the number of child-generated materials is high; this indicates the level of children's participation in communication. Clearly displayed print supports the process, since nonreadable print can't communicate effectively. Display space and materials support communication, since the amount of shared personal communication that can be posted is limited to available facilities for display.

Book Use

There are three categories in the survey that identify encouragement for the use of books. The information from this group describes the extent environmental arrangements emphasize valuing and enjoying books. Included in this group are *books related to nearby materials, objects, or pictures; different kinds of books*; and *presence of books with cover or page displayed.*

All the arrangements in this group are designed to foster the use of books and reflect the assumption that part of being literate is being a reader of books. The variety and patterns of distribution show how well the environment provides arrangements of books to interest every child.

Comparing Category Groups

It is sometimes interesting to look for the relative emphasis on different literacy contexts and other qualities by comparing the group scores for each category. However, the group scores are not directly comparable. The summary totals for some categories are derived from counted stimuli; others include uncounted categories and could not show as high a score because of the way the information is originally recorded.

The value of the summary by category groups is that it highlights the complexity of the literacy environment and describes some of the contextual literacy available for children's participation. In combination with the specific data about areas and categories on the record sheet, the summary data offer a way to seek answers for important questions about the functioning literacy environment:

How much are children participating in this environment?
Is it what the teacher intended?
Does the environment encourage different purposes for literacy?
Is there a stimulus for literacy everywhere?
Are there all kinds of literacy, so everyone has the chance to practice all forms?
What literacy possibilities have been overlooked?

The analysis of environmental literacy through The Survey of Displayed Literacy Stimuli is part of an ongoing process of adapting the environment to meet children's changing learning needs and interests. The process begins with an examination of the environment to determine its capacity to support children's learning activity, and it includes analysis for literacy and for the other special purposes teachers have chosen to promote through environmental arrangements. This process leads to environmental reorganization, which is also the beginning of a new cycle, leading to further analysis.

APPENDIXES

GENERAL REFERENCES

INDEX

The Survey of Displayed Literacy Stimuli

EXHIBIT 1. SURVEY COVER PAGE/DIRECTIONS

The Survey of Displayed Literacy Stimuli can help determine the level of stimuli and support for spontaneous literacy behaviors in a learning environment. The Survey examines each area for information about the *pattern of distribution* of the literacy stimuli in the environment and compares one area to another. The Survey also shows the *kinds* of literacy stimuli offered within areas and within the whole environment.

How to Use the Survey

1. **Look at the classroom.** Make a sketch map of your classroom environment, showing its spatial organization. Divide the total into different areas, deciding boundaries, space, and materials for each. Include *all* classroom space in these areas. List each area at the top of the survey record.
2. **Survey one area at a time.** Enter an area and sit so you can see all displayed materials from child's eye level. Begin the examination with the category definitions beside the survey record. *Count only those materials displayed at children's eye level or below.* Complete the recording for all literacy stimuli categories in one area before moving to the next area.
3. **Count one category of literacy stimuli at a time.** With the category definitions beside the survey record, count all visible literacy stimuli in a given category. *Recheck the definitions for each category when you are ready to count.*

   Look first at the category, then examine the area for items that belong in that category. Remember, you are searching for items that fit in a category; you do not try to find a category for each item you see. Record the number of instances in one category by tally or numeral before going on to the next category. Remember that *only* displayed items, at child's eye level or below, are counted.
4. **Yes or no categories.** The last five categories on the survey are not counted. Recheck the category definition. Then examine the area for presence of the stimuli described and record its presence or absence.

Source: C. Loughlin & N. Cole. (1986, May).

5. **Total.** To compare one area of the environment with another, total each column. This will show where the stimuli for literacy are in the entire environment.

To compare the relative emphasis on different categories of literacy stimuli, total the records across each row. This will show the variety of stimuli and support for literacy behaviors in the environment.

EXHIBIT 2. SURVEY RECORDING SHEET

Each item must be clearly visible and within child's eye level/range. Definitions attached.

	DISPLAYED LITERACY STIMULI	AREAS									Total by Category
Record Actual Count	1. current child-generated messages, labels, stories.										
	2. messages about the current day.										
	3. displayed directions for activity.										
	4. sign-on charts or sheets.										
	5. different kinds of books.										
	6. different kinds of recording tools.										
	7. different kinds of recording materials.										
	8. different references.										
	9. print or writing segments related to nearby materials, objects, pictures.										
	10. books related to nearby materials, objects, or pictures.										
	11. community culture/language books or print segments.										
Record 1 or 0 (Yes or no)	12. presence of empty display space.										
	13. presence of display tools.										
	14. presence of clearly legible displayed handwritten or machine print segments.										
	15. presence of books with cover or page displayed.										
	16. presence of functional labels.										
	TOTAL PER AREA										

Date ____________ Special Conditions ____________

Number of areas surveyed ____________

Classroom and Grade Level ____________ Observer ____________

EXHIBIT 3. SURVEY CATEGORY DEFINITIONS

Each item must be clearly visible, and at child's eye level or below.

1. **Current child-generated messages, labels, or stories (less than five days old):** These may be child-written or child-dictated. Determined by dated material or by asking. Groups of completed assignments displayed together are excluded. Items in this category may also be counted in other categories.
2. **Messages about the current day:** Schedules, assignments, notices, groupings, news, and announcements needed to work through the day. These are clearly related to events on the day of the survey.
3. **Displayed directions for activities:** Displayed tasks, cards, or charts that give directions for activities or procedures that children can carry out independently. Labels that explain how to operate equipment or care for material are excluded.
4. **Sign-on charts or sheets:** Teacher- or child-prepared charts or sheets, clearly displayed, that call for children to record information in print or symbol, or to sign names.
5. **Different kinds of books:** The number or different kinds of books available for children's access, displayed so they are clearly visible (i.e., trade, reference, child-made, magazines, etc.). The number of volumes is *not* counted.
6. **Different kinds of recording tools:** The number of different kinds of tools for children's use in recording events, ideas, information (i.e., pencils, crayons, chalk, tape recorders, etc.). Duplicates in an area are *not* counted.
7. **Different kinds of recording materials:** The number of different kinds of materials for children to record upon (i.e., audiotape, stationery, chart paper, chalkboard, drawing paper, etc.). Duplicates in an area are *not* counted.
8. **Different references:** Lists, pictures, charts, or other information sources children may use as references to help with ongoing activities. A set of references (i.e., encyclopedia) stored together is counted as one reference. Single volumes placed in different locations are counted. Duplicates in an area are *not* counted.
9. **Print or writing segments related to nearby materials, objects, or pictures:** Print placed close to pictures or other materials, with the contents of the print or writing clearly related to those materials in some way. Labels are excluded. Children's illustrated stories are excluded, unless they are related to other nearby materials.
10. **Books related to nearby materials, objects, or pictures:** Books located in combination with other materials, objects, or pictures, and whose contents are clearly related to those materials in some way.
11. **Community culture/language books or print segments:** Books and print segments written in children's home language, or reflecting home culture, in a fairly homogeneous linguistic/cultural community not ordinarily represented in educational materials.

12. **Presence of empty display space:** Empty space in the area that is clearly available for children to display their own work. This is not always labeled and can be determined by indications that materials have been displayed there, by something already displayed but not using all the space, or by asking.

13. **Presence of display tools:** Visibly displayed tacks, tape, label blanks, and/or other tools children can use to display materials.

14. **Presence of clearly legible handwritten or machine-printed segments:** Print and child or teacher writing, displayed on unpatterned background with empty space surrounding the print segment. Print or writing is large enough to be seen by children in the area.

15. **Presence of books with cover or page displayed:** Books in the area with the covers clearly visible, displayed, or with a particular page clearly visible.

16. **Presence of functional labels:** Working labels on holders, cabinets, or equipment that give information about contents, use, or procedures for use.

EXHIBIT 4. SURVEY SUMMARY SHEET

Observer_____ Date _____ Classroom _____ Grade/Age _____

AREAS

No. areas surveyed   _____

No. areas with all 1-10
categories   _____

No. areas with all 12-16
categories   _____

No. areas with category 11 _____

CATEGORIES

No. 1-11 categories in
environment   _____

No. 12-16 categories in
environment   _____

Functional Score

Categories:

2 _____
3 _____
4 _____
8 _____
16_____

T_____

Child-generated Score

Category:

1_____

Communication Score

Categories:

1 _____
12_____
13_____
14_____

T_____

Variety Score

Categories:

5_____
6_____
7_____
8_____

T_____

Content Score

Categories:

9 _____
10_____
11_____

T_____

Book Use Score

Categories:

5 _____
10_____
15_____

T_____

TOTALS

Categories 1-11 score   _____

Categories 12-16 score   _____

Environmental Evidence for Literacy Growth

Just as it is possible for the environment to stimulate and support literacy, it is possible to use the environment to analyze some aspects of children's literacy growth. The products and the behaviors within the environment provide information about learning and attitudes that pupils have internalized; about the use of literacy in the work context of the day's activities; and about the use of various literacy-related skills.

There are two sources of environmental evidence regularly available for consideration: 1) the products of children's activities, and 2) the glimpses of children involved in literacy practices throughout the day. It is appropriate to keep in mind that only certain aspects of all the literacy learning and application are visible in the environment; the emphasis here is on what can be observed.

The following checklist presents a series of questions about reading behaviors that teachers often ask about children's growth; it identifies elements of the environment and pupils' behavior that can be examined; and it lists the chapters that can be referred to for more information.

1. Do the children know how to use reference books and resources?

Read the environment for:

Alphabetized filing of children's materials	5
Work-in-progress stored with references	7
Location of encyclopedia volumes at end of day	2, 7, 9
Use-worn vocabulary references	6, 8
Worn and fingerprinted reference charts	2, 6, 8
Dog-eared directories and catalogues	2, 9
Accurate spelling in edited writing	8
Accurate punctuation in edited writing	8

Note children in the environment:
    Glancing toward alphabet cards 3, 8
    Using shared word banks 8
    Asking others for reference information 7, 8
    Looking at information sources 2, 7, 9
    Responding to others' requests about references 6, 7, 8
    Helping others find a dictionary item 7, 8
    Reading information to others from references 7, 8, 9
    Using references together 7, 9
    Using books for help with projects 7, 9

2. Do children read aloud with meaning?

Read the environment for:
    Sign-on sheets for reading volunteers 5, 9
    Sign-on audiences for volunteer readers 9
Note children in the environment:
    Volunteering to find and read aloud needed information 5, 7
    Reading a committee report to a group 7, 8
    Reading creative writing to friends or co-workers 8
    Reading to entertain a group 9
    Using good inflection in reading dramatic roles 7, 8

3. Are children aware of different purposes for writing?

Read the environment for:
    Child-written work in committee reports 7
    Original stories, poetry, and other literary forms 8
    Daily and personal messages, lists, tallies, etc. 5, 6
    How-to instructions written by pupils 5
    Charts, diagrams, and other nonnarrative communication 7
    Pupil-constructed maps 7
    Written announcements of current events 5, 7
    Posted announcements of recurrent events 5
    Requests for special information or supplies 5, 6
    Inventories or budget lists for special projects 5
    Science experiment reports 7, 8
Note children in the environment:
    Writing a response to a friend 6
    Writing a request to teacher or classmates 6
    Making work reports in some written form 5, 7
    Keeping logs, journals, or other personal writing 8
    Producing instructions 5
    Making sign-on charts 5, 6, 7, 8, 9
    Writing various literary forms: poetry, plays, fiction,
      nonfiction 7, 8

4. Do children understand what they read?

Read the environment for:
Posted or filed research summaries	7
Research notes of work-in-progress	7, 8
Responses to sign-ons	5, 6, 7, 8, 9
Responses to requests for information, assistance, etc.	5, 6
Answers to personal messages	6
Book suggestions or criticisms	9
Posted opinions or arguments	8
Letters to authors	8
Examples of work made by following printed instructions	5
Products indicating use of recipes, diagrams	7
Use of rule books or instruction books	9

Note children in the environment:
Responding to posted schedules, announcements, routines	5
Making choices announced only in print	5
Responding to personal messages	6
Using recipes, construction diagrams, etc.	5, 7
Following display directions accurately	3, 5
Using instruction manuals	9
Using rule books	9

5. Do children recognize and use writing conventions?

Read the environment for:
Samples showing level of knowledge of left-to-right, top-to-bottom order	3, 5, 6, 7, 8, 9
Samples showing improvement in legibility	3, 5, 6, 7, 8, 9
Work-in-progress, showing revision effort	8
Samples showing editing marks	8
Samples of final edited drafts	8
Levels of punctuation competencies	3, 5, 6, 7, 8, 9
Levels of spelling development	3, 5, 6, 7, 8, 9
Punctuation information charts showing use	8
Spelling references showing regular use	8
Samples revealing knowledge of grammar	3, 5, 6, 7, 8, 9

Note children in the environment:
Beginning and continuing use of page placement conventions	6, 7, 8
Looking for accurate models	8
Using source materials for assistance in using conventions	8
Asking peers/adults for help	6, 7, 8
Using punctuation guidance in oral reading	9
Editing work to improve conventions	8

6. Do children show an ability to figure out new words?

Read the environment for:
Examples of new vocabulary in written products	7, 8
Examples of appositive use of definitions	7, 8

Note children in the environment:
Looking up new words encountered in reading	7, 9
Sounding out syllables accurately in oral reading	7, 9
Analyzing prefixes, endings, or roots in strange words	5, 7, 9
Asking peers for help in pronouncing or understanding	5, 7, 9
Using known objects to help decode accompanying print text	5, 7, 8, 9

7. Do children choose a variety of reading materials?

Read the environment for:
Types of books kept in individual storage	9
Change in variety of books displayed in environment	9
Posted reports of books read	9
Sign-on sheets for use of various books	7, 9
Library request lists	7, 9
Suggestions for classroom book purchases	7, 9
Personal books brought from home	9

Note children in the environment:
Using book resources with objects or activities	3, 7, 8, 9
Checking out books for personal use	9
Using various types of resources in project work	7
Using books to support personally selected work	7, 8, 9

8. Given a chance, do children elect to read books?

Read the environment for:
Presence of books among personal possessions	9
Volunteered reports or information about books	9
Reference to books in reported work	7
Products or activities based on book information	7, 8, 9

Note children in the environment:
Using books for recreation during free time	9
Sharing books with classmates	9
Carrying nonassigned books home	9

9. Do children use a variety of writing/study skills?

Read the environment for:
Written summaries of factual information	7

Written summaries in book reviews	9
Source material, rewritten to accompany display	7, 8, 9
Research information summarized to share with work group	7
Outlines filed with written work-in-progress	7, 8
Contrast and comparisons of information	7, 9
Materials reflecting good sequencing ability	5, 7, 8, 9
Statements of hypothesis guiding work	7
Questions about projects or conclusions	7
Statements about implications and inferences	7, 8, 9

Note children in the environment:

Rewriting research material	7
Providing summary notes for group reports	5, 7
Taking notes during lessons or film	7

10. Do children write for record-keeping?

Read the environment for:

Child-written record of absences	5
Tallies of classroom business, other information	5
Food and water records about animals and plants	5
Notes about classroom science projects	5, 7

Note children in the environment:

Making records of ongoing class projects	5, 7
Recording results of experiments	7, 8

11. Do children write for a variety of purposes in learning activities?

Read the environment for:

Listing of current events	5, 7
Requests for special information or supplies	5, 7
Inventories of materials	5
List of class or project expenses	5, 7
Displayed film and book reviews	7, 8, 9
Histories, biographies, community documents	7, 8
Weather reports	5, 7
Feeding and watering records	5

Note children in the environment:

Writing and displaying schedules for current events	5
Producing lists for field trips	5, 7
Planning budgets needed for special activities or purchases	5
Keeping records of experiments	7
Taking class notes	7, 8
Outlining/summarizing information	7, 8
Making diagrams	7

12. Do children write/read for social purposes?

Read the environment for:
Invitations	6
Personal messages	6
Shared projects	5, 7, 8
Committee lists for social activities	5, 6
Committee reports for social activities	5, 6
Announcements of personal news	6

Note children in the environment:
Using writing to report group work	7, 8
Writing personal requests and responses	6
Writing/reading personal messages	6
Exchanging phone numbers	6
Exchanging addresses	6
Writing letters	6
Making special-event cards	6

13. Do children write functional announcements and instructions?

Read the environment for:
Child-written recipes, construction directions, patterns, outlines	5
Child-written sign-ons for clean-up tasks	5
Child-written anouncements	5

Note children in the environment:
Writing instructions for a cooperative construction project	5
Sharing a recipe	5

14. Are children aware of different literary forms?

Read the environment for:
Children's products in a variety of styles: fiction, poetry, explanations, descriptions, etc.	8
Books of varied literary styles in regular use	9

Note children in the environment:
Using books of varied literary styles	9
Writing in a variety of literary forms	8

15. Do children show awareness of standard grammar/syntax?

Read the environment for:
Growth toward standard punctuation	5, 6, 7, 8
Growth toward standard spelling	5, 6, 7, 8
Consistency in tenses within a product	5, 6, 7, 8
Agreement of subject/verb	5, 6, 7, 8

General References

Alberty, B., & Weber, L. (1979). *Continuity and connection: Curriculum in five open classrooms.* New York: City College of New York, Workshop Center for Open Education.

Baghban, M. (1984). *Our daughter learns to read and write.* Newark, DE: International Reading Association.

Boyer, E. L. (1983). *High school: A report on secondary education in America.* New York: Harper & Row, Publishers.

Burnett, F. H. (1962). *The secret garden.* New York: J. B. Lippincott.

Calkins, L. M. (1983). *Lessons from a child: On the teaching and learning of writing.* Portsmouth, NH: Heinemann Educational Books.

Cazden, C. B. (1972). *Child language and education.* New York: Holt, Rinehart & Winston.

Clark, M. (1976). *Young fluent readers: What can they teach us?* London: Heinemann Educational Books.

Clark, R. C., Moran, P. R., & Burrows, A. A. (1981). *The ESL miscellany: A cultural and linguistic inventory of American English.* Brattleboro, VT: Pro Lingua Associates.

Clay, M. (1972). *Reading: The patterning of complex behavior.* London: Heinemann Educational Books.

Clay, M. (1975). *What did I write?* Aukland, New Zealand: Heinemann Educational Books Ltd.

Clay, M. (1982). *Observing young readers: Selected papers.* Exeter, NH: Heinemann Educational Books.

Coates, G. (Ed.). (1974). *Alternative learning environments.* Stroudsberg, PA: Dowden, Hutch & Ross.

Cole, N., & Loughlin, C. (1984). The survey of displayed literacy stimuli. In B. Ivener & C. Loughlin (Eds.), *Final report: Literacy content of classroom environments and children's literacy behaviors* (pp. 14–16). Unpublished report, Albuquerque Public Schools, Albuquerque, NM.

Collins, M. (1984, November). *A literacy environment for kindergarten.* Paper presented at Young Children and Literacy Meeting, Albuquerque, NM.

David, T., & Wright, B. (Eds.). (1974). *Learning environments.* Chicago: University of Chicago Press.

177

Dean, J. (1974). *Room to learn: Working space, language areas, and a place to paint.* New York: Citation Press.

DeFord, D. E. (Ed.). (1980). Learning to write: An expression of language [Special issue]. *Theory into Practice, 19*(3).

Durkin, D. (1966). *Children who read early.* New York: Teachers College Press.

Egan, J. (1981, November). Thirty-two going on eight. *Insights, 14*(3), 1–7.

Egoff, S., Stubbs, G. T., & Ashley, L. F. (1980). *Only connect.* Toronto: Oxford University Press.

Engel, B. (1973). *Arranging the informal classroom.* Newton, MA: Education Development Center.

Ferreiro, E., & Teberosky, A. (1979). *Literacy before schooling.* Exeter, NH: Heinemann Educational Books.

Fisher, C., & Terry, C. A. (1982). *Children's language and the language arts* (2nd ed.). New York: McGraw Hill.

Flood, J., & Lapp, D. (1981). *Language/reading instruction for the young child.* New York: MacMillan Publishing Co.

Georgiou, C. (1969). *Children and their literature.* Englewood Cliffs, NJ: Prentice-Hall.

Gere, A. R., & Smith, E. (1979). *Attitude, language and change.* Urbana, IL: National Council of Teachers of English.

Goelman, H., Oberg, A., & Smith, F. (1984). *Awakening to literacy.* Exeter, NH: Heinemann Educational Books.

Golub, L. (1975). Stimulating and receiving children's writing: Implications for an elementary writing curriculum. In R. Larson (Ed.), *Children and writing in the elementary school* (pp. 70–87). New York: Oxford University Press.

Goodman, K. (1977). Acquiring literacy is natural: Who skilled Cock Robin? *Theory into Practice, 16*(5), 309–314.

Goodman, K. (1981). *Language and literacy: The selected writings of Kenneth S. Goodman, Vol. I: Process, theory, research.* Boston: Routledge & Kegan Paul.

Goodman, K. (1982). *The selected writings of Kenneth S. Goodman, Vol II: Reading, language and the classroom teacher.* Boston: Routledge & Kegan Paul.

Graves, D. (1983). *Writing: Teachers and children at work.* Exeter, NH: Heinemann Educational Books.

Hall, M. A. (1981). *Teaching reading as a language experience* (3rd ed.). Columbus, OH: Charles E. Merrill.

Halliday, Michael A. K. (1973). *Explorations in the functions of language.* London: Arnold.

Harste, J., Woodward, V., & Burke C. (1984). *Language stories and literacy lessons.* Portsmouth, NH: Heinemann Educational Books.

Hart, R. (1979). *Children's experience of place.* New York: Irvington Publishers.

Henderson, E. (1981). *Learning to read and spell: The child's knowledge of words.* DeKalb: Northern Illinois University Press.

Holdaway, D. (1979). *The Foundations of literacy.* Sydney, Australia: Ashton Scholastic.

Holdaway, D. (1980). *Independence in reading: A handbook on individualized procedures.* Exeter, NH: Heinemann Educational Books.

Holdaway, D. (1984). *Stability and change in literacy learning.* Exeter, NH: Heinemann Educational Books.

Huck, C. S. (1976). *Children's literature in the elementary school* (3rd ed.). New York: Holt, Rinehart & Winston.

Hughes, M. M. (1975). *The professional response: How teachers become important to children.* Unpublished manuscript, University of New Mexico, College of Education, Albuquerque.

Ivener, B. (1983). Inservice: A teacher-chosen direction for creating environments for literacy. *The New Mexico Journal of Reading, 3*(2), 7–12.

Jewell, M. G., & Zintz, M. V. (1986). *Learning to read naturally.* Dubuque: Kendall Hunt Publishing Company.

Jones, E., & Prescott, E. (1984). *Dimensions of teaching learning environments: A handbook for teachers in elementary schools and day care centers* (2nd ed.). Pasadena, CA: Pacific Oaks College Bookstore.

Kent, S. (1984). *Analyzing activity areas: An ethnoarcheological study of the use of space.* Albuquerque: University of New Mexico Press.

King, M. G., & Marans, R. W. (1979). *The physical environment and the learning process: A survey of recent research.* Ann Arbor: University of Michigan, Institute for Social Research.

King, R. (1982). The nature and teaching of writing: A generative diagram. *Insights, 15*(4), 1–8.

Krashen, S. D., & Terrell, T. D. (1983). *The natural approach: Language acquisition in the classroom.* San Francisco: The Alemany Press.

Kritchevsky, S., Prescott, E., & Walling, L. (1977). *Planning environments for young children: Physical space* (2nd ed.). Washington: National Association for the Education of Young Children.

Lee, D., & Van Allen, R. (1963). *Learning to read through experience.* New York: Appleton-Century-Crofts.

Lindfors, J. (1985). Understanding the development of language structures. In A. Jaggar & M. T. Smith-Burke (Eds.), *Observing the language learner* (pp. 41–65). Newark, DE: International Reading Association.

Loughlin, C. E. (1977). Understanding the learning environment. *The Elementary School Journal, 78*(2), 126–131.

Loughlin, C. E. (1978). Arranging the learning environment. *Insights, 11*(2), 1–5.

Loughlin, C. E. (1982). Reflecting literacy in the environment. *New Mexico Journal of Reading, 3*(1), 17–19.

Loughlin, C. E., & Ivener, B. L. (1984, February). *Literacy content of kindergarten-primary environments and children's literate behaviors: Prelimi-*

nary report. Paper presented at North Dakota Study Group on Evaluation, Racine, WI.

Loughlin, C. E., & Cole, N. The survey of displayed literacy stimuli. (1986, May). Albuquerque: University of New Mexico.

Loughlin, C. E., & Suina, J. H. (1982). *The learning environment: An instructional strategy.* New York: Teachers College Press.

Loughlin, C. E., & Suina, J. H. (1983). Reflecting the child's community in the classroom environment. *Childhood Education, 60*(1), 18–21.

Loughlin, W. A. (1976). Integrating indoor and outdoor education . . . with a camera. *The Communicator, 7*(2), 12–15.

Lux, D. (Ed.). (1986). Building literacy [Special issue]. *Theory into Practice, 25*(2).

Martin, M. D. (1974). *Reading information to children.* Unpublished manuscript. Albuquerque: University of New Mexico, College of Education.

Martin, M. D. (1979). *Valuing reading.* [Monograph]. Grand Forks, ND: University of North Dakota, Follow Through Program.

Martin, M. D. (1982). Community. *Insights, 14*(5), 1–6.

Martin, M. D., & Loughlin, C. E. (1976). A dynamic teacher role. *Journal of Teaching and Learning, 2*(2), 34–44.

Moffett, J. (1973). *A student-centered language arts curriculum, grades K–6: A handbook for teachers.* Boston: Houghton Mifflin Co.

Olson, W. (1952, Spring). Seeking, self-selection and pacing in the use of books by children. *The Packet, 7*(1), 1–6.

Ortiz, L., & Loughlin, C. (1986). Curriculum building with children. *AYCE Junge Kinder, 16*(6), 21–26.

Osman, L. (1971). *Patterns for designing children's centers.* New York: Educational Facilities Laboratory.

Parker, R., & Davis, F. (Eds.). (1983). *Developing literacy: Young children's use of language.* Newark, DE: International Reading Association.

Piaget, J. (1971). Development and learning. In J. Raths, J. R. Pancella, & J. Van Ness (Eds.), *Studying teaching* (2nd ed.), (pp. 283–296). Englewood Cliffs, NJ: Prentice-Hall.

Proshansky, H., Ittelson, W. H., & Rivlin, L. G. (Eds.). (1970). *Environmental psychology.* New York: Holt, Rinehart & Winston.

Rambusch, N. M. (1971, November). *Helping children become self-directive and self-selective.* Paper presented at the Annual Conference of the National Association for the Education of Young Children, Minneapolis.

Read, C. (1975). Lessons to be learned from the preschool orthographer. In W. Lenneberg (Ed.), *Foundations of language development: Vol. 1. A multidisciplinary approach.* Paris: The UNESCO Press.

Rubin, Z. (1980). *Children's friendships.* Cambridge, MA: Harvard University Press.

Schickendanz, J. A. (1986). *More than the ABC's: The early stages of reading and writing.* Washington: National Association for the Education of Young Children.

Sheehan, P., & Cole, N. (1983). How to look at environments to see what literacy support there is. *New Mexico Journal of Reading, 3*(2), 11–13.

Smith, F. (1978). *Reading without nonsense.* New York: Teachers College Press.

Smith, F. (1978). *Understanding reading: A psycholinguistic analysis of reading and learning to read* (2nd ed.). New York: Holt, Rinehart & Winston.

Smith, F. (1983). *Essays into literacy.* Exeter, NH: Heinemann Educational Books.

Sommer, R. (1974). *Personal space: The behavioral basis for design.* Englewood Cliffs, NJ: Prentice-Hall, Inc.

Stewing, J. W. (1983). *Exploring language arts in the elementary classroom.* New York: Holt, Rinehart & Winston.

Sutton-Smith, B. (1970). The playful modes of knowing. In S. Arnaud & N. Curry (Eds.), *Play: The child strives toward self-realization* (pp. 32–46). Washington: National Association for the Education of Young Children.

Taba, H. (1968). *A teacher's guide to elementary social studies.* Boston: Addison-Wesley.

Taylor, D. (1983). *Family literacy: Young children learning to read and write.* Exeter, NH: Heinemann Educational Books.

Temple, C., Nathan, R., & Burris, N. (1982). *The beginnings of writing.* Boston: Allyn & Bacon, Inc.

Tovey, D. R., & Kerber, J. E. (Eds.). (1986). *Roles in literacy learning.* Newark, DE: International Reading Association.

Van Dongen, R. (1983). *Building experience.* Unpublished manuscript. University of New Mexico, Department of Elementary Education, Albuquerque.

Van Dongen, R. (1984). Stretching the literary experience. *Insights, 17*(4), 1–6.

Veatch, J. (1959). *Individualizing your reading program.* New York: G. P. Putnam's & Son.

Walberg, H. J. (1979). *Educational environments and effects.* Berkeley, CA: McCutcheon Publishing Corporation.

Yanamoto, K. (Ed.). (1979). *Children in time and space.* New York: Teachers College Press.

Index